PARENTING SKILLS

BASED ON THE QUR'AN AND SUNNAH
[With Practical Examples for various Ages]

Drs. Ekram & Mohamed Rida Beshir

amana publications

First Edition
2004 A.C./1425 A.H.

Second Printing
2007 A.C./1427 A.H.

amana publications
10710 Tucker Street,
Beltsville, MD 20705 USA
Tel: (301) 595-5999
Fax: (301) 595-5888
Email: amana@igprinting.com
Website: amana-publications.com

Library of Congress Cataloging-in-Publication Data

Beshir, Ekram.
Parenting skills : based on the Qur'an and Sunnah [with practical examples for various ages] / Ekram & Mohamed Rida Beshir.
p. cm.
Includes bibliographical references.
ISBN 1-59008-029-7
1. Child rearing–Religious aspects–Islam. 2. Parenting–Religious aspects–Islam. I. Beshir, Mohamed Rida. II. Title.

HQ769.3.B473 2004
649' .1–dc22

2004019500

Printed in the United States of America by
International Graphics
10710 Tucker Street
Beltsville, MD 20705
Tel: (301) 595-5999
Fax: (301) 595-5888
E-mail: ig@igprinting.com
Website: igprinting.com

PARENTING SKILLS

BASED ON THE QUR'AN AND SUNNAH

Contents

ACKNOWLEDGMENT

We would like to express our sincere gratitude to our good friend, Jennifer Templin, for all the time and hard work she put into editing this book. We will be forever indebted to her for her gracious support and dedication to this work. May Allah bless her, keep her on the Straight Path and reward her with *jannah*.

We kindly request that every reader make *du'a* for her.

Drs. Ekram and Mohamed Rida Beshir

Preface

For all of those parents who attended our positive parenting skills workshops over the last few years, who blessed us with their *du'a*, who enriched our workshops with their intelligent questions and wonderful feedback, and who asked us to put the workshop material into a written format to make it available as a reference that could benefit others as well, this is a humble attempt to fulfill your request.

We have written this book as a supplement to the many parenting workshops that we have given over the years. When giving workshops, we find that the time is never enough to cover all of the relevant principles and to provide enough examples to clearly explain the concepts to everyone. Therefore, in writing this book, we have added some principles and taken into consideration the many thoughtful questions that parents have asked us, to include more concrete examples. We have also tried to keep this book short and simple to make it accessible to the average parent, whose free time is often limited.

We pray that Allah accept this effort from you and from us, make our deeds for His sake alone, keep us all on the Straight Path, and reward us all with *jannah, insha'Allah.*

INTRODUCTION

Everyone realizes that raising children is a very important task for many reasons. Some of these reasons are listed below:

• ... Our children are a trust from Allah *SWT*. Allah entrusted us with them and we will be held accountable for how we carried out and whether we fulfilled this trust. The Prophet Muhammad *SAAW* said:

"كفى بالمرء إثما أن يضيع من يعول"

"It is enough sin for a person to let those who depend on him go astray."[1]

Also, Allah SWT said in the Qur'an:

"إِنَّا نَحْنُ نُحْيِي الْمَوْتَى وَنَكْتُبُ مَا قَدَّمُوا وَآثَارَهُمْ وَكُلَّ شَيْءٍ أحْصَيْنَاهُ فِي إِمَامٍ مُبِينٍ"

"We are recording what they presented and also their influences, and We have counted everything in a clear and manifest record."[2]

Knowing how much children are influenced by their parents, we can see that this verse applies to us as parents. Children are a product of the influence that their parents have on them and Allah is going to ask parents about that influence on Judgment Day.

• ... Children contribute a great deal to their parents' happiness. Even if a parent had all the material means to be happy, such as money, a career, or successful investments, these material things would not make her happy, if one of her children were to go astray.

1. Mustadrak

2. (Q36, V12)

- ... Children are our biggest investments. It is quite unfortunate that many parents are investing more time, energy and money on various materialistic endeavors than on their children. We should look at our children as the men and women of the future and we should see that time spent with them is not wasted time. It is very well invested time. Imagine, if even a small proportion of Muslims were to look at their children as an investment and treat them as such, if they were to spend enough time with their children to make sure they were behaving properly and acquiring the right Islamic concepts about life, and if they could touch their hearts and souls with the beauty of Islam, then we would *insha'Alla*h have a much stronger community and the situation of Muslims would certainly be better.

Knowing the objectives of *tarbiyah*, having a strong knowledge of the basic principles of parenting according to the Qur'an and *sunnah,* performing the Self-Search process to change oneself as a parent, and putting these principles into practice are the key factors in enabling parents to acquire positive parenting skills and provide the most effective and efficient parenting methods for their children. This is the primary focus of this book.

The objective of *tarbiyah*, as we indicated in the first chapter of our book, *Meeting the Challenge of Parenting in the West, An Islamic Perspective*, is to ensure that our children grow up to be happy and righteous people who understand their role in this life. We want to help them have high self-esteem and a strong enough character to be able to face the challenges ahead of them in this society. We also want them to possess certain important qualities that are essential to making them feel proud as Muslims.[3] In the following few pages, *insha'Allah,* we will discuss the Self-Search process in detail, with practical examples, and then follow up with various Islamic parenting principles. In addition, we will provide several examples of how parents can implement these principles

3. See chapter one of *Meeting the Challenge of Parenting in the West, an Islamic Perspective,* Third Edition, by Drs. Ekram and M. Rida Beshir, Amana Publications, 2003.

with their children of various ages. With this, *insha'Allah*, we hope that parents will be equipped with the tools needed to raise their children in the most effective and positive way.

A note about the writing

Italicized words are Arabic words and phrases commonly used by Muslims.

The structure (Qx, Vy) refers to the yth verse of the xth chapter of the Qur'an. For example, (Q2, V7) denotes the 7th verse of the 2nd chapter of the Qur'an

There are many collections of the sayings (*ahadith*) of the Prophet *SAAW*. In this book, we quote from many of those collections, but primarily from the following six: Bukhari, Muslim, Abu Dawud, Nisai, Tirmidhi, and Ibn Majah. The *ahadith* in this text are followed by a footnote indicating which collection the *hadith* was taken from.

The expression *agreed upon* means that the *hadith* was reported by both Bukhari and Muslim.

The abbreviation *SWT* is used after the name of Allah, and it stands for *subhanahu wa ta'ala*, which means "glory be to Allah, the Exhalted."

The abbreviation *SAAW* is used after the name of the Prophet Muhammad, and it stands for *sallallahu 'alayhe wasallam*, which means "may Allah's peace and blessings be upon him."

The abbreviation AS is used after the name of other prophets and it stands for *'alayhe salaam, which means "may Allah's peace be upon him."*

The abbreviation *RAA* is used, usually after the name of one of the Prophet's *SAAW* companions who narrated his sayings. It stands for *radiyallahu 'anhu* or *'anha*, which means "may Allah be pleased with him or her."

The pronouns *he* and *she*, and *him* and *her* are alternated throughout the text to maintain a balance in referring to both men and women.

English translations of the Arabic quotations have been adapted for the modern reader.

CHAPTER 1

SELF-SEARCH

The origin of Self-Search in Islam is the concept of *mohasabah*. It is a very important concept in Islam and it comes from the following verse:

"يَا أَيُّهَا الَّذِينَ آمَنُوا اتَّقُوا اللَّهَ وَلْتَنظُرْ نَفْسٌ مَّا قَدَّمَتْ لِغَدٍ وَاتَّقُوا اللَّهَ إِنَّ اللَّهَ خَبِيرٌ بِمَا تَعْمَلُونَ"

"O you who believe, remain conscious of Allah (have *taqwa*), and let every human being look to what he has sent ahead for the morrow. And once again, remain conscious of Allah (have *taqwa*), for Allah is fully aware of all that you do."[4]

The Prophet *SAAW* also emphasized that we should always assess and evaluate our actions and deeds. In fact, he labelled the person who does not do this as *ghafel* or *a'jez*, which means careless, complacent, and unable. Shaddad Ibn Awes *RAA* narrated that the Prophet *SAAW* said:

"الكيس من دان نفسه وعمل لما بعد الموت والعاجز من أتبع نفسه هواها ثم تمنى على الله"

"A wise person is one who blames himself for his short-comings and works hard for what comes after death, while a careless and complacent person (*ghafel*) or unable person (*a'jez*) is one who follows his whims and desires and keeps hoping for the mercy of Allah."

Omar Ibn al-Khattab *RAA* used to say:

4. (Q59, V18)

"حاسبوا أنفسكم قبل أن تحاسبوا، وزنوا أعمالكم قبل أن توزنوا، فإن أهون عليكم في الحساب غدًا أن تحاسبوا أنفسكم اليوم ، وتزينوا للعرض الأكبر "يومئذٍ تعرضون لا تخفى منكم خافية"

"Review, evaluate, and assess yourself before you are assessed. Weigh your deeds before they are weighed against you, and prepare yourself for the day where you will be fully exposed."[5]

Al-Hassan al-Basry *RAA* used to say:

"المؤمن قوام على نفسه، يحاسب نفسه لله، وإنما خف الحساب يوم القيامة على قوم حاسبوا أنفسهم في الدنيا، وإنما شق الحساب يوم القيامة على قوم أخذوا هذا الأمر من غير محاسبة"

"Believers observe themselves and maintain their good deeds. They always review, assess, and evaluate their status. Those who do this in life will have an easy time on the Day of Judgment. And those who do not, will have a difficult time on the Day of Judgment."

The following is reported in the tablets of Ibraheem:

"ينبغي للعاقل ما لم يكن مغلوباً على عقله أن يكون له أربع ساعات ساعة يناجي فيها ربه ، وساعة يحاسب فيها نفسه ، وساعة يتفكر في صنع الله ، وساعة يخلو فيها لحاجته من المطعم والمشرب"

"A wise person should divide her time into four portions; one portion to supplicate to her Lord, a second portion to review, evaluate, and assess herself, the third portion to reflect upon the creation of Allah, and the fourth portion to work and earn her living."[6]

---

5. Ahmad

6. Ibn Hibban and Hakim

We should remember that one day we will be fully exposed, as Allah *SWT* says in *Surah al-Haqqah:*

"يَوْمَئِذٍ تُعْرَضُونَ لَا تَخْفَىٰ مِنكُمْ خَافِيَةٌ"

"On that day, you will be exposed to view, no secret of yours will remain hidden."[7]

Therefore, it is a wise practice for believers to assess and review their actions regularly. Relationships can be enhanced if actions are monitored and changed as soon as faults are discovered. Scholars recommend that a process of *mohasabah* be implemented to help improve and enhance the level of our *taqwa* and closeness to Allah. This process should be done frequently to achieve the best possible results. It requires that parents assess their actions, first as individuals, then together as a couple. They should have a list of questions to ask themselves, maybe at the end of the day or at the end of the week. This list of questions should cover their daily activities with their children, as well as characteristics and behaviour, such as worship and interaction with others. This will help the parents evaluate how good their days are and discover whether they have room for improvement. The following are examples of questions that their list should include:

- Did I perform my daily prayers on time?
- Did I donate money and charity for the sake of Allah?
- Did I think about what I wanted to say before speaking?
- Did I hurt the feelings of my fellow humans in any way?
- Did I express my love and appreciation for my children and family members?
- Did I thank my spouse for his or her efforts in helping me with the children?
- Did I speak nicely about my family members?
- Did I treat my children kindly?
- Did I.... ?

7. (Q 69, V 18)

This is just a sample of the questions that all Muslims should ask themselves to evaluate their performance during that specific day or week. If the answers are positive, we should be thankful to Allah *SWT*. If we realize that there are shortcomings in our performance, we should make a strong commitment to correct our mistakes and perform better in the future.

Parents can do a lot to improve their parenting skills through the Self-Search process. This process helps parents instill certain great qualities in their children that will help them become strong and confident Muslims who can resist the temptations around them. The Self-Search process can also help parents ensure that they themselves have these qualities as well. If parents do not have positive qualities, they will not be able to instill any in their children. Such qualities can only be acquired through hard work that starts with an honest and sincere **SELF-SEARCH**, to make sure that what parents say and do has the proper impact on their children to support and motivate them. It helps children build a strong, balanced personality, have a positive outlook on life, and be confident that they can have not only a positive impact on their surroundings but also a profound one. With such characteristics children will be able to take what is good and leave what is bad, and even influence the society they live in. They can steer it in the right direction by exercising proper moral values for their own well-being and for the well-being of the generations to come.

Parents should follow these six steps to implement the Self-Search process:

SEARCH
EVALUATE
ACKNOWLEDGE
REINFORCE
CHANGE
HANG ON

Search within ourselves and review all the actions and parental behaviours that we use with our children. We must dig deep into our past, thinking back to childhood, and uncover any hidden reasons that might be the source of our parental behaviour. Often, we may be talking to our children in a certain way, and if we stopped to think about it, we would realize that we are doing exactly what our mom or dad used to do with us. The following questionnaire will help us in the **searching** process.

Answer the following questions as best as you can and be honest with yourself.

During my childhood and my teen years:

1. (a) I felt that my parents loved me because they told me verbally and through hugs and kisses.
   (b) My parents didn't say that they loved me and/or they did not hug and kiss me, but I could feel their love indirectly at times.
   (c) I didn't feel my parents' love and doubted that they loved me at all.
2. (a) I felt that my parents were interested in me and that they took my personal affairs seriously, despite their busy schedules.
   (b) I felt that my parents did not pay much attention to my personal affairs. I often felt like my parents did not treat me as if I had a distinct personality from the rest of my siblings.
   (c) I didn't get any attention at all from my parents.
3. (a) I felt my parents' encouragement and support and they helped me whenever they could.
   (b) I didn't feel my parents' encouragement and support and they didn't help me when they could have
4. (a) I felt my parents' approval and knew that they took my efforts seriously no matter what the results were.
   (b) I didn't feel my parents' approval unless I took on more than I could handle to meet their expectations.
   (c) I didn't feel my parents' approval no matter what I did.

5. (a) My parents were strict with me and expected me to take on responsibilities.
   (b) My parents were not always strict with me and did not always expect me to take on responsibilities.
   (c) My parents were never strict with me and didn't expect me to do anything.
6. (a) My parents often compared me with my siblings or other kids we knew, which made me very sad.
   (b) My parents appreciated me as I was.
7. Write the name of someone who had a positive effect on you during your childhood and growing years.
8. Is this person one of your parents?
9. Write the name of someone who had a negative effect on you during your childhood and growing years.
10. Is this person one of your parents?

Evaluate the actions and sayings we use in dealing with our children. Which of these actions are positive, supportive, and based on Islamic values and teachings, and which of these actions are negative, unsupportive, and have no basis in Islamic teachings? An example of a negative action is when we, as parents, try to resolve a conflict with our child while we are angry. If we yell, shout, and fight with the child just to vent our anger, we are using a negative parental behaviour. However, if we control our anger by using the anger management techniques prescribed to us by our beloved Prophet *SAAW*, teach our child to do the same, and then discuss the problem calmly, we are using a positive parental behaviour. We will present more examples of positive and negative parental behaviours after we complete the Self-Search process. The following is another questionnaire that will help in the process of **evaluation**.

Please answer the following questions with "yes" or "no."

As a parent:

1. I feel that I had little experience with my first child. This caused me to be too strict or too lenient with him or her.
2. I expect perfection of myself when I am with my children and I often feel like a failure when I can't do the perfect thing.
3. I feel that cleaning the house and preparing the food is more important than playing with my children or taking them to the park.
4. I don't often let my children try certain things that I think are difficult, because I wasn't able to do them when I was a child.
5. I feel that I'm raising my children in the same way that my parents raised me, despite the difference in time and place. This is because I don't know of a better way to raise them.
6. The way I treat my children shows that I don't have confi dence in their ability to do things.
7. I let my children make simple decisions that are specific to them and reasonable for their age.
8. I feel that the stress and new responsibilities of adapting to a new environment, as an immigrant, are a heavy burden on my spouse and I. They don't leave us enough time to meet the needs and wants of our children.

Acknowledge our findings after we answer the above questions, and categorize them as either positive or negative behaviours. Again, the positive ones are those that agree with Islamic teachings, are suitable for the environment, and help our children become strong and confident Muslims. The negative behaviours are those that are mainly from inherited tradition, have no basis in Islamic teachings, may not be suitable for the environment, and may make our children feel defeated as Muslims. Acknowledging our strengths and weaknesses is the first step in improving our parental behaviour. After that, we have to put our trust in Allah *SWT* and make a commitment to positive change. Changing unhealthy habits is the key to success, as the great scholar, Ibn al-Qayyim said:

"وملاك الأمر كلة فى خلع العادات"

"And the core of the matter is in leaving out the unhealthy, inherited habits."

Reinforce the positive parental behaviours and keep practicing them with our children. If they work, we must continue using them

Change the negative parental behaviours and replace them with positive ones. We have to work hard at this because change does not come easily. It takes hard work to change habits, so we have to be patient and keep trying. Changing bad habits into good ones is worth the struggle. The expected benefits in our children's development are too important for us not to try our best to change these habits. When trying to change our bad habits or negative parenting behaviour, we should follow the advice of the Prophet *SAAW* and always perform *salat-ul-hajah*, the prayer of need, and make *du'a* intensively, to help us in the process of trying to become a better parent. In addition, we must repeat this prayer a few times, rather than just performing it once.

Hang On: We cannot give up right away. We should put our trust in Allah and keep trying. As parents, we can learn new ways and improve on our old ways. The positive results will be certain if we follow the above steps. It may take longer than we think, but we can't give up. The reward will be tremendous if we work hard and make a sincere effort to become better parents.

Finally, we would like to remind parents that changing behaviour is a long process that requires patience, endurance, persistence, and sincerity. It is something that takes time to achieve. You may have to go through this process a few times, but don't give up. Set a reasonable goal for yourself, try your best to achieve it gradually, put your trust in Allah, pray often, and make a lot of *du'a* asking for His support. The results, *insha'Allah*, will be certain.

Examples of positive and negative parental behaviours

The following examples can be found in various areas of raising children, starting with the little comments and nicknames that parents casually say to their children and covering the more serious matters such as parents' responses to disrespect from their children.

• **Positive and negative comments**

– Suppose your son is helping you set the table for dinner and you tell him, "I love the way you are helping me." **This is a positive parental behaviour.**

– Suppose your daughter is wearing a new dress and you make the comment, "That looks nice on you." Again, **this is a positive parental behaviour.**

– Note: Parents should make positive comments such as these in response to specific, positive behaviours or actions from their children. Parents should not simply praise their child continuously if the child has not made any effort. Parents must take advantage of specific events or actions that their children do, to say something positive to them.

– On the other hand, suppose your son is helping you set the table and he accidentally drops a glass, and you say, "You are always clumsy like that." **This is a negative parental behaviour.**

– Suppose you call your children names, or insult them by saying things such as, "She's a little troublemaker," or "He's as skinny as a stick." **This is a negative parental behaviour.**

• **Responding to disrespect**

– Islam promotes respect in all relationships; it is a very important part of the Muslim personality. However, our children are surrounded by a culture that does not promote respect. Our children are affected by this culture and may sometimes respond to their parents and to other elders in the community in a disrespectful way. Parents have to correct this behavior. If they correct it in the proper way, using a proven, successful method (**Indicate, Educate, and Train**),[8] **this is a positive parental behaviour.** However, if they ignore this behaviour or correct it in a harsh way by yelling or shouting, or in a humiliating way by correcting the child in front of her siblings or friends, **this is a negative parental behaviour.**

• ***Hayaa'***

– *Hayaa'* means decency, modesty, bashfulness, morality, and humility. It is a very important, noble, and cherished characteristic in Islam, to the extent that the Prophet *SAAW* said:

"لكل دين خلق وخلق الإسلام الحياء"

> "There is a characteristic for every deen (religion), and the characteristic of Islam is *hayaa*'"[9]

Unfortunately, the culture surrounding our children does not promote this concept. As a matter of fact, popular culture promotes the exact opposite through TV shows, movies, commercials, magazines, and lyrics in music, which all have a strong influence on the way people dress and behave in public. Again, our children are affected by this culture and may, on some occasions, behave in a way that does not reflect hayaa'. Parents have to correct this behaviour as well. If they correct it in the proper way, with a proven, successful method (**Indicate, Educate, and Train**),[10] **this is a positive parental behaviour**. However, if they ignore this behaviour or correct it in a harsh way by yelling or shouting, or in a humiliating way by correcting the child in front of his siblings or friends, **this is a negative parental behavior.**

---

8. The **Indicate, Educate, and Train** technique is described in detail at the end of this chapter.

9. Al-Isaba, Version 1.06

10. The **Indicate, Educate, and Train** technique is described in detail at the end of this chapter.

• **Friends and Acquaintances**

– Children need friends in their lives to interact and build relationships with. If parents recognize and acknowledge this need, help fulfill it, and explain the proper criteria for selecting those friends to their children, **this is a positive parental behavior**. If parents simply don't pay attention to this need, are indifferent about it, and think that it is enough for their children to interact with their siblings, **this is a negative parental behavior**.

• **Providing a positive lifestyle**

– It is very important to provide a positive lifestyle for our children, especially since we live here in the West. This will help them not to feel inferior to other children their age. This way, when they grow up and are on their own, *insha'Allah*, they won't feel that their youth was robbed from them and that they want to rush to experiment with things that may be unacceptable from an Islamic point of view. If parents understand this clearly, and provide an active and positive lifestyle for their children at home, in the community, and in society, **this is a positive parental behavior**. If parents are indifferent about this, and neglect providing a positive lifestyle to their children, **this is a negative parental behavior**.

The Indicate, Educate, and Train technique

This is a recommended Islamic method of correcting and changing a child's negative behaviour. It consists of three steps:

1. **Indicate** clearly to the child her mistake or unacceptable behaviour in a very calm but firm manner. For example, if the child was disrespectful, by speaking to an older person in a rude tone of voice or by making faces at the person she was talking to, the parent who is dealing with the situation should assume that the child didn't know better, and then indicate to her that this behavior

is not acceptable. Do this by using an appropriate comment that suites the child's age, and with a firm tone of voice that is calm and not angry. It is important to emphasize here that this should be done in a very respectful way, to set an example and to show the child how you want her to behave.

2. **Educate** the child about the issue at hand using verses from the Qur'an and teachings of the Prophet Muhammad *SAAW*. For example, when responding to disrespect, the parent could mention the following saying of the Prophet Muhammad *SAAW*:

"ليس منا من لم يرحم صغيرنا ويوقر كبيرنا"

"The one who does not have mercy on our young ones and does not show respect to our elders is not one of us."[11]

When talking about *hayaa'*, parents could use the following verse from the Qur'an:

"إِنَّ السَّمْعَ وَالْبَصَرَ وَالْفُؤَادَ كُلُّ أُولَـٰئِكَ كَانَ عَنْهُ مَسْؤُولاً"

"You are responsible and will be asked about what you hear, what you see, and what goes through your heart."[12]

Suppose that you and your children are watching TV and an indecent scene comes on the screen. Tell them to turn it off and remind them that Allah will hold us accountable for everything that we hear and see. Do not ignore such situations because it is going to stay in the mind of the child. You have to comment on it in the proper way and tell them that this is something we should not participate in or even observe, because we will be held accountable for it, as Allah *SWT* has told us.

11. Tirmidhi

12. (Q17, V36)

Using verses from the Qur'an and the teachings of the Prophet *SAAW* helps the child understand that our ultimate reference is to the orders of Allah *SWT*, and that even parents are expected to adhere to these orders. This will also help parents avoid confrontations with their children. It removes the factors that cause power struggles, since the parents are not making up the rules and imposing them on the children, but actually, both the parents and children are following Allah's rules. It is also important to indicate here that, for parents to be able to **educate** properly, they must be knowledgeable about the verses of the Qur'an and the sayings of the Prophet Muhammad *SAAW* that are related to the various manners and concepts that they want to instill in the hearts and minds of their children. The Islamic literature that is available on this subject is indeed plentiful. A book by Sheikh Muhammad Al-Ghazali called *The Muslim Character*, and a book by Sheikh Abdel-Fatah Abu Ghodah called *Islamic Manners* are two very good sources on this subject. Complete information about these books is listed in the reference section at the back of this book.

3. **Train** the child to frequently practice the correct behaviour in the proper way, with your guidance. Do not expect that, by following these steps once, the child will behave appropriately all the time and not repeat the mistake. You need to repeat the process each time the child repeats the mistake or behaves in an unacceptable way. You may have to do it more than once until it becomes a habit for the child. Training and practice make perfect.

CHAPTER 2

UNDERSTAND YOUR CHILD

The principle of understanding your child comes from the fact that Islam bases everything on knowledge. The first verse of the Qur'an that was revealed deals with the most important tool of acquiring knowledge:

"اقْرَأْ بِاسْمِ رَبِّكَ الَّذِي خَلَقَ"

"Read in the name of your Lord, who has created [human]."[13]

In the first five verses of this revelation, Allah *SWT* uses the words *iqra, 'allama, and al-qalam,* which translate into *read*, *taught*, and *pen*, respectively. These are all tools used to acquire knowledge. In addition, all scholars agree that, in order for our acts of worship to be accepted, they must be performed for the right reasons, and based on proper knowledge. For example, when dealing with our children, we must have a thorough understanding of the issue at hand in order to properly and adequately address it with them. If we want to know how to motivate our children to function in a useful and cooperative way, we must have some understanding of the psychological mechanisms involved

All human actions have a purpose. This applies to both adults and children. The purpose may be known or unknown to us. As parents, knowing this hidden purpose will enable us to help our children behave differently by changing their motives. Two main motives drive the actions of children. These are, the need to belong and the need for attention.

---

13. (Q96, V1)

The need to belong is a basic need for children, as it is for adults. A child feels secure when she has a place in a group, family, or class at school. Beginning in infancy, a child will explore ways to find her place in the family. Any person will feel that he belongs to a certain community or group if he has something in common with the other members of that group. Common activities create bonds between the people who share them. For a child to satisfy such needs in the school environment, she has to take part in some activities with her peers. This participation will ensure that she has something in common with classmates. A common mistake that some parents, who are being cautious, make is in failing to give their children permission to be part of any extra-curricular activities. This deprives the child of satisfying her need to belong at school. **A better way of being cautious** is for parents to help their children identify the activities that do not conform to Islamic etiquette and stay away from them. Parents should also help their children select some school activities that are not specifically for Muslims only, such as being a member of the street patrol team or the school computer club.

Another way to help your child satisfy this need is to allow him to watch significant events on special occasions, such as when the local basketball team is playing in the finals, when the city hockey team makes it to the playoffs, or when the Olympics or the World Cup are on TV. Allowing the child to watch part of one of these events will give him something to talk about with his peers at school the next day. We would like to emphasize, however, that the child should not be allowed to sit in front of the TV watching the entire game or series, because this is a waste of time. Allowing him to watch a brief segment such as the last quarter of a basketball game or the last period of a hockey game, or part of one specific Olympic event, will be enough to satisfy his need, give him something to talk about with his peers, and still allow him to use his time wisely.

Seeking attention is another basic need of children. Children will repeat any action that brings them attention and will abandon actions that make them feel left out. All children do this without even realizing it.

Parents must know that children need to feel that they are being noticed and not ignored. If a child is playing nicely and quietly and nobody notices, she will try to attract attention through fights and mischief. A child would rather be noticed as a bad child than be ignored as a well-behaved one. Parents should reward their children's positive behaviour with attention and ignore their negative behaviour.

Example

If a young child is colouring quietly in his room, Mom or Dad should occasionally check on him and say some words of encouragement such as, "*Masha'Allah*, you have been colouring this nice picture on your own. This is beautiful. I really like this." Such comments will encourage the child to continue engaging in such positive activities. In addition, parents should always ignore trivial, negative behaviour from the child so that he will not repeat it.

Example

Three-year-old Hasan frequently goes to the kitchen, opens the fridge door, and looks inside the fridge for a few seconds. As soon as he does this, his mom usually shuts the fridge door and yells at him, "Hasan, how many times do I have to tell you not to open the fridge door?" Hasan will continue to repeat the same behaviour because he is getting his mother's attention by doing it. Rather than shouting and yelling at him, his mother should ignore the negative behaviour, as long as he is not making a mess or putting himself in danger. In addition, she should make a mental note that her son may be bored, which may be why he keeps opening the fridge door. She should try to find an activity for him to occupy his time.

Sharp Observation

Another important quality of children that parents should take note of is their outstanding ability to observe things around them.

Children are expert observers, but they make many mistakes in interpreting what they observe.

Example

Take the case of an older child resorting to baby-like behaviour because of the attention the family is giving to her newborn sibling. The child is a very good observer, noticing all the attention given to the baby, but she draws the wrong conclusion and chooses an incorrect way of trying to find her place in the family. The parents can correct this behaviour by giving the older child their attention while involving her in helping out with the new baby's care, and praising her for this help. Praising the child for her help and making her feel that she is capable of helping her parents is very important for the emotional well-being of the child. It promotes a sense of security and reduces her feeling that the new baby is a threat to her.

Reaction to Obstacles

Parents must also understand how children react when faced with an obstacle, such as a temporary or permanent physical handicap, a learning disability, or a move to a new and unfamiliar environment. Children who have gained courage from positive and supportive methods of training work hard to compensate for and overcome these obstacles. They do not easily give up or get discouraged. They discuss any problems from their outside environment with their parents, in an effort to collectively find a solution. They try their parents' suggestions one after another, or come up with their own suggestions and try them until the problem is solved. However, children who do not have support from home, to give them courage, give up when they face obstacles. Either they do not mix with others, or they always follow the crowd regardless of whether the crowd is right or wrong.

To help our children react to obstacles, it is very important to provide them with love, support, and continuous encouragement. We must not be critical of them when they seek our help in discussing one of the problems they are facing. We must suspend our judgment, listen to them attentively and share their feelings. This way *insha'Allah,* we will strengthen their ability to overcome any problems that they may face and we will contribute positively to their strong personalities.

Key Factors Affecting Children's Personalities

Scholars identify the following three factors as the most important factors affecting the formation of a child's personality: Family atmosphere, position within the family, and training methods. Let us now discuss these in detail

Family Atmosphere

The family is the child's first environment and it has a significant impact on the child's personality. The relationship between the parents sets a pattern for all other relationships in the family. If parents deal with each other in a respectful, loving, and merciful way, tolerate each other, show each other care and gentleness, all those beautiful qualities will set the standard for every family member and will be reflected in the child's personality.

Disciplining the children is a shared responsibility. The father should not undermine the mother's orders by disagreeing with her decision on a disciplinary matter. If the parents disagree, the father should first discuss the matter with the mother in private. This should never be done in front of the children. In our interactions with Muslim families during parenting workshops and at Islamic conferences, we have witnessed two extremes. At one extreme are the fathers who insist that they have nothing to do with the children's upbringing and do not help the mother at all; they even hinder good training by undermining the mother's orders in front of the children. At the other extreme are the mothers who do nothing useful with their children all day long and, when the children do something that requires her attention, she tells them to wait until their father comes home. Both of these attitudes are wrong. *Tarbiya* is a joint responsibility and both spouses should be involved in the process. They should establish a clear *tarbiya* plan that is studied, well thought out, and agreed upon between them. *Tarbiya* should not be left unplanned. Parents should lead the *tarbiya* train, rather than being led by their children's behaviours into one reaction after another.

Children observe and absorb the family's attitude toward spending money, toward achievement and effort, toward success and contribution, toward other races, and toward differences.

Being fair in dealing with our children, and not favouring one of them over the other, contributes positively to their personalities and is important for a healthy family atmosphere.

Cooperation between parents and family members is another positive quality that helps children develop healthy personalities.

Moderation in everything enhances a balanced personality.

The importance of early religious training is well recognized. This is why practicing Islam in front of the children, involving them, and providing an Islamic atmosphere at home is essential to linking children with Allah *SWT*.

Children experience society at large through their relationship with their parents. In every family, children will have certain common characteristics and children are the expression of the family atmosphere. However, all children from one family are not necessarily the same.

Position of the Child Within the Family

The dynamics associated with the child's position within the family is another important factor that influences her personality. As we indicated before, the child is on a continuous search to fit into, and find her place in, the family. For example, in a family that consists of a husband, wife, and one child, this child always enjoys a lot of attention from her parents. She is the first child and the only child, and all the family time that the parents have is mainly for her. She primarily interacts with two adults and generally receives more than she gives. When a second baby arrives, he represents a threat to the first child. The dynamics are now different for the first one. She is now the older of the two children and the baby is the newcomer who receives more attention. But the baby is in a different position than the first child was when she was a newborn, because he already has an older sibling. The older child is now observing all the attention given to the baby and, based on the family atmosphere, she will interpret this attention in her own way.

A competition is now starting for the parents' attention and the first child has to find her new position within the family. If the family atmosphere is encouraging, the child will adjust, or establish a new position, as the child who is being helpful and who can contribute more than the baby. If the child gets discouraged, she will give up, might resort to misbehaving, and find her position as the bad child in the family, as long as it gets her the attention she needs.

With the birth of every child after that, the dynamics change and each child has to re-establish his position within the family. One child may choose to be the achiever, while another may choose to be the helpless one. A third may go for the pleasing personality, the helping one or the bad one. Whichever position the child takes, it may form lifelong attitudes and habits.

The parents' cooperation is essential to ensure that each new child finds her place within the family in the most peaceful and painless way. When parents are knowledgeable and realize the importance of working together to improve the situation, they can help the child find a useful position in the family.

Methods of Training

Methods of training used by parents to bring their children up properly are the third factor that affects a child's personality. The methods used to train a child have a great impact on his personality. If the methods used are strict and not balanced, the child's personality will not be moderate and he might select extreme views in his adult life. If the methods are not accompanied by practical examples, the child will recognize contradictions between his parents' words and actions and will not take their instructions seriously in the future. There are basic principles, as well as Islamic methods, of tarbiyah, deduced from the Qur'an and the teachings of Prophet Muhammad *SAAW*, that parents have to observe when applying any method of training. These principles include: linking the child to Allah; being merciful, gentle, kind and lenient; emphasizing the child's positive actions; using clear communication; being fair; helping the child develop skills; and providing better alternatives to the things they do not want their children to do. As for the Islamic methods of training, leading by example and providing a role model are at the top of the list. Others include giving gentle advice, offering rewards and punishment, building habits, using events,utilizing time properly, telling stories, and playing games.[14] It is important for parents to understand the influence that these methods have on their children's personalities so they can be careful about what they do with their children.

---

14. See chapter 4 of our book *Meeting the Challenge of Parenting in the West, An Islamic perspective.*

CHAPTER 3

LINK THE CHILD TO ALLAH

The concept of linking our children to Allah is a very important concept for Muslims. It is a continuous process that begins with the birth of the child. The instruction of the Prophet *SAAW* is to make the *adhaan*—the call to prayer—in the child's right ear, and the *iqamah* in the child's left ear, right after birth. This way, the first word they hear is the name of Allah *SWT*. From then on, parents should always make sure that the child is hearing the name of Allah, the recitation of the Qur'an, *tasbeeh*, regular prayers and supplications even if the child is very young and does not understand their meaning. Parents should take their children with them to the juma'a prayers. After prayer, parents can put their children on their laps and make the end-of-prayer *tasbeeh* on the childrens' hands.

Parents must try to present a positive, protecting and loving image of Allah *SWT* to their children, and not in a threatening or frightening way. Unfortunately, some parents always paint a picture of Allah *SWT* as a punishing God by what they say and by how they say it. For example, some parents tell their young child, "If you don't do such-and-such a thing, Allah will put you in the hellfire." Even worse, some parents repeat this threat to their children over and over during the day. This is an incorrect approach that paints the wrong picture of Allah *SWT* in children's minds. Young children are easily frightened. Therefore, it is more appropriate and better to talk to them about Allah positively, saying such things as, "Allah loves you because you helped your sister," or "Allah loves you because you perform your prayers." Even when children do something inappropriate, parents can still comment with a positive portrayal of Allah *SWT*. For example, if a child is pushing her sister, a parent can say, "Allah knows that you can play nicely with your sister and He loves to see you sharing."

When their children are very young, parents should concentrate on Allah's kind, merciful, and gentle attributes when they talk to their children. This does not mean that they should not mention that Allah will punish those who do evil deeds. It just means that the emphasis should be on the rewarding and forgiving attributes of Allah *SWT*. As the children grow older, parents can talk more about punishment and fear of Allah *SWT*.

Telling stories of the life of the Prophet *SAAW* and emphasizing the fact that Allah *SWT* supports the believers are effective ways to link the child to Allah *SWT* and make him feel that Allah is with him all the time. Some of these stories include how Allah *SWT* protected his Messenger *SAAW* during migration from Makkah to Madinah, and the one about how Allah *SWT* supported the believers during the battle of Badr.

Reciting verses from Qur'an that illustrate the concept that Allah *SWT* loves the believers and supports them also helps link the child to Allah *SWT* in a positive and loving way. An example of such a verse is the last verse of chapter 16:

"إِنَّ اللَّهَ مَعَ الَّذِينَ اتَّقَواْ وَّالَّذِينَ هُم مُّحْسِنُونَ"

"Certainly Allah is with those who exercise *taqwa* and those who do *ihsan*."[15]

Other examples are in the following verses:

"وَاللَّهُ يُحِبُّ الْمُحْسِنِينَ"

"And Allah loves those who do *ihsan*."[16]

"إِنَّا لَنَنصُرُ رُسُلَنَا وَالَّذِينَ آمَنُوا فِي الْحَيَاةِ الدُّنْيَا وَيَوْمَ يَقُومُ الْأَشْهَادُ"

15. (Q16, V128)
16. (Q3, V134)

> "We will, without doubt, help Our messengers and those who believe in this world's life and in the Day when witnesses will stand forth."[17]

Parents should help set up situations to make the child feel that Allah *SWT* is helping her. One opportunity to do this is when the child misplaces something. Parents should help the child find it while they are making the prayer for lost items:

"اللهم يا جامع الناس ليوم لا ريب فيه اجمع بيني وبين ضالتي"

> "Oh Allah, the One who has the power to resurrect evryone on a sure day, help me find my lost object."

When she finds her belonging, this will have a great impact on her, knowing that Allah *SWT* helps her. If she does not find the missing object, it gives parents an opportunity to introduce the concept of *du'a* and how Allah *SWT* responds to *du'a* in different ways.

Parents should make sure that the child understands that authority belongs to Allah *SWT*; even parents are subject to His authority. This can only be achieved with practical examples and by practicing what they preach to the child, such as praying, fasting, telling the truth, and being helpful. Parents should put their children in situations where they will see that other people are also performing such deeds and actions and they are also subject to Allah's authority. Parents can do this by visiting other Muslim families and by participating in activities at the mosque and in other Islamic events with their children.

17. (Q40, V51)

CHAPTER 4

MERCY, KINDNESS, AND GENTLENESS

Mercy is the essence of Islam. Allah *SWT* tells His Messenger, Muhammad, *SAAW*:

"وَمَا أَرْسَلْنَاكَ إِلَّا رَحْمَةً لِّلْعَالَمِينَ"

"We have sent you as a mercy for all creatures."[18]

In another verse, He tells him:

"فَبِمَا رَحْمَةٍ مِّنَ اللّهِ لِنتَ لَهُمْ وَلَوْ كُنتَ فَظّاً غَلِيظَ الْقَلْبِ لاَنفَضُّواْ مِنْ حَوْلِكَ فَاعْفُ عَنْهُمْ وَاسْتَغْفِرْ لَهُمْ وَشَاوِرْهُمْ فِي الأَمْرِ فَإِذَا عَزَمْتَ فَتَوَكَّلْ عَلَى اللّهِ إِنَّ اللّهَ يُحِبُّ الْمُتَوَكِّلِينَ"

"Had you been stern and harsh-hearted, they would have dispersed from around you."[19]

It was also narrated by Abu Hurairah that:

الأقرع بن حابس أبصر النبي صلى الله عليه وسلم يقبل الحسن. فقال: إن لي عشرة من الولد ما قبلت واحدا منهم. فقال رسول الله صلى الله عليه وسلم "إنه من لايرحم لا يرحم"

"Al-Aqra' Ibn Habes, of the Bedouin, saw the Prophet *SAAW* kissing his grandson, and he said, 'I have ten children; I have never kissed any one of them.' The Prophet *SAAW* said, 'Allah will not have mercy on a person who does not have mercy on others.'"[20]

---

18. (Q21, V107)
19. (Q3, V159)
20. Muslim

Parents should deal with each other, and with their children, in a way that reflects this mercy. This does not mean that they cannot be firm with their children. Parents can maintain both mercy and firmness while implementing *tarbiya* with their children. Children should also see and feel a merciful relationship between their parents. They should see it in the way the parents treat each other and help each other. They should not detect the least bit of harshness in their parents' relationship. Husbands should help their wives in various things related to the house, especially things related to *tarbiya* with the children. The Prophet Muhammad *SAAW* used to be seen helping his family in their household chores. It was reported that he told his righteous companions:

"خيركم خيركم لأهله، وأنا خيركم لأهلي"

"The best of you is the one who is best with his family, and, among you, I am the best to my family."[21]

Unfortunately, it is quite customary among some husbands from Eastern countries to leave all of the children's matters to their wives. Many husbands tell their wives, "The children are your responsibility." This is not the right attitude. Similarly, some wives may neglect their children's needs all day long, until the husband comes home from work. This attitude is also not correct because it is not one of cooperation and does not reflect any mercy. Raising the children is a responsibility that must be shared by both husband and wife and should be done by both of them in a well-planned and studied manner. A relationship based on mercy among the various family members creates a very positive environment that is conducive to better *tarbiyah*

Here are some more **examples** that illustrate the mercy of the Prophet *SAAW* toward children:

---

21. Al-Jame' Al-Sagheer

It was narrated by Ibn Asaker that the Messenger of Allah *SAAW* said:

"من كان له صبي فليتصابى له"

"And whoever has a child should act like a child with him or her."[22]

• He also used to line up Abdullah, Ubaidoallah and Kothair, the sons of Alabas, and ask them to run toward him, saying, "Whoever wins the race, I'll give him such-and-such." They used to come running and jump up to hug him, and he would kiss them.

• Al-Tabarani also reported that Abu Hurairah said that the Prophet *SAAW* took his grandson, al-Hasan's, hand and put his feet on the Prophet's feet and told him to "climb up."

• In *Sahih Muslim,* Jabir *RAA* narrated that he saw the Prophet *SAAW* crawling on his hands and knees while al-Hasan and al-Hussein were riding on his back, and he used to say:

"نعم الجمل جملكما! ونعم العدلان أنتما"

"The best riders are you and the best camel is yours."

• It was reported that Anas *RAA* said:

"ما رأيت أحدا كان أرحم بالعيال من رسول الله صلى الله عليه وسلم"

"I have never seen anybody who is more merciful with children than the Prophet *SAAW*."

22. Al-Jame' Al-Sagheer

• Anas also reported that whenever the Prophet *SAAW* passed by children on the road, he would smile at them and say salaam to them.[23]

• The Prophet *SAAW* also said:

"ليس منا من لم يرحم صغيرنا ويوقر كبيرنا"

"The one who does not have mercy on our young ones and does not show respect to our elders is not from among us."[24]

• It was narrated that the Prophet *SAAW* said:

"إنه من لايرحم لا يرحم"

"Allah will not have mercy on the one who has no mercy on others."[25]

• 'A'isha *RAA* (beloved wife of the Prophet *SAAW*) reported that the Messenger of Allah *SAAW* said:

"إن اللّه رفيق يحب الرفق في الأمر كله"

"Allah is kind and gentle. He loves kindness in all affairs."[26]

• She *RAA* also reported that the Messenger of Allah *SAAW* said:

"إن اللّه رفيق يحب الرفق، ويعطي على الرفق ما لا يعطي على العنف وما لا يعطي على ما سواه"

"Allah is kind and He loves kindness, and He grants to those who are kind that which He does not grant to those

23. Bukhari and Muslim
24. Tirmidhi, Ahmad, and Hakim
25. Muslim
26. Agreed upon

who are severe and does not grant anything to those who use anything else besides it (kindness)."[27]

• 'A'isha *RAA*, the mother of the believers, reported that the Messenger of Allah *SAAW* said:

"ما كان الرفق في شيء إلا زانه، ولا نزع من شيء إلا شانه"

"Kindness is not found in anything, but it adds beauty to it, and if it is withdrawn from anything, it defects it."[28]

• Jareer ibn Abdullah *RAA* reported that he heard the Messenger of Allah *SAAW* saying:

"من يحرم الرفق يحرم الخير كله"

"The one who is deprived of leniency is deprived of all good."[29]

• Ibn Abbas *RAA* reported that he heard the Messenger of Allah *SAAW* saying to Ashaj Abdul Qais *RAA*:

"بك خصلتان يحبهما الله: الأناة والتؤدة"

"You possess two qualities that Allah loves. These are forbearance and leniency."[30]

• It was also reported on the authority of Abu Hurairah *RAA* that a Bedouin man urinated in the mosque and some people rushed to beat him up. Thereupon, the Messenger of Allah *SAAW* ordered them to leave him and pour a tumbler of water over the spot that

---

27. Muslim
28. Al-Jami' al-Sagheer
29. Muslim
30. Muslim

he urinated on to wash it out. Then the Prophet *SAAW* said, "You [the Companions of the Prophet] have been sent to make things easy and not to make them difficult."[31]

• Allah *SWT* also describes the Prophet *SAAW* as the most kind and merciful to the believers at the end of *Surah al-Tawbah*[32]:

"لَقَدْ جَاءَكُمْ رَسُولٌ مِّنْ أَنفُسِكُمْ عَزِيزٌ عَلَيْهِ مَا عَنِتُّمْ حَرِيصٌ عَلَيْكُم بِالْمُؤْمِنِينَ رَؤُوفٌ رَّحِيمٌ"

> "Now a Messenger has come to you from amongst yourselves. It grieves him that you should receive any injury or difficulty. He is anxious over you (to be rightly guided, to repent to Allah and beg Him to pardon and forgive your sins in order that you may enter Paradise and be saved from the punishment of the Hellfire). He is the most kind a merciful to the believers."

All of the above verses from the Qur'an and *ahadith* emphasize the importance of kindness and gentleness in relationships with other human beings. They are wonderful qualities for parents to have. These qualities help tremendously in parents' dealings with their children and make the process of *tarbiya* much easier.

To illustrate the kindness of the Prophet *SAAW*, let us look at his manners. Even when he was giving advice to someone, he was very considerate and would use the best wording, especially with young people. It was narrated that when Jabir was young, the Prophet *SAAW* advised him on the proper manners of eating, by saying, "O my dear son, mention the name of Allah and eat with your right hand and eat from the closest part of the dish to you." Notice that he *SAAW* used the phrase, "*Ya bonay*" (O, my dear son) as if the child were his own son. The Qur'an also uses the same phrase for the advice of Luqman to his son:

---

31. Bukhari
32. (Q9, V128)

"وَإِذْ قَالَ لُقْمَانُ لِابْنِهِ وَهُوَ يَعِظُهُ يَا بُنَيَّ لَا تُشْرِكْ بِاللَّهِ إِنَّ الشِّرْكَ لَظُلْمٌ عَظِيمٌ"

"'Behold,' Luqman said to his son by way of gentle advice. '*O my dear son*, in worship, do not join others with Allah, for false worship is indeed the highest wrongdoing.'"[33]

The Prophet *SAAW* used a similar phrase when he was advising Ibn Abbas that if he adheres to the orders of Allah *SWT* and safeguards the commandments of Allah, Allah will be with him, supporting and protecting him. On that occasion, Ibn Abbas was riding behind the Prophet *SAAW*, as reported by al-Tirmidhi. The Prophet *SAAW* began his advice with the expression, "*Ya-Ghulam*," which is a gentle phrase used to describe preteens and young teenagers.

All of the above examples have a great lesson in them for parents to follow. Unfortunately, some parents deal with their children in a very harsh way, especially when their children make mistakes. Being gentle, kind and using a merciful but firm tone of voice when instructing your child has at least four benefits:

1. You are rewarded for following the Prophet's *SAAW* example.
2. It always brings better results, according to the above sayings of the Prophet *SAAW*.
3. Your child will feel that you love him and want the best for him, not that you are just venting your anger at him.
4. It keeps the channel of communication open between you and your child, which is very important during your child's teenage years.

Example

One example of when you can use mercy and gentleness with your children, and this particularly applies to fathers, is when you

33. (Q31, V13)

come home at the end of the day. Usually, the father is tired after a long day at work, especially with the added stress of driving to and from work in rush-hour traffic. Therefore, most fathers arrive home in a very bad mood with a frowning face. Our advice to all fathers is, before entering your house, stay in your car, in the driveway, for few minutes, making *tasbeeh*, and reciting or listening to verses of the Qur'an to calm down and forget about the hectic day you had. This will help put you in the right mood to enter your home with a positive attitude and a big smile on your face. Hug your children and kiss them as soon as you enter, spend some time with them and ask them about their day. Just 10 to 15 minutes with your children while you are in a good, gentle, and merciful mood will work wonders, keeping a good relationship and a strong bond between you and your children.

CHAPTER 5

TEACH THEM RESPECT

Being kind and merciful to children does not mean that you should let them behave disrespectfully toward their parents, in particular, or toward others, in general. The Prophet *SAAW* said:

"ليس منا من لم يرحم صغيرنا ويوقر كبيرنا"

> "The one who does not have mercy on our young ones and does not show respect to our elders is not from among us."

The glorious Qur'an emphasizes, in so many places, the importance of showing respect for both parents. In *Surah al-Israa'*, Allah *SWT* says:

"وَقَضَى رَبُّكَ أَلاَّ تَعْبُدُواْ إِلاَّ إِيَّاهُ وَبِالْوَالِدَيْنِ إِحْسَاناً إِمَّا يَبْلُغَنَّ عِندَكَ الْكِبَرَ أَحَدُهُمَا أَوْ كِلاَهُمَا فَلاَ تَقُل لَّهُمَا أُفٍّ وَلاَ تَنْهَرْهُمَا وَقُل لَّهُمَا قَوْلاً كَرِيماً * وَاخْفِضْ لَهُمَا جَنَاحَ الذُّلِّ مِنَ الرَّحْمَةِ وَقُل رَّبِّ ارْحَمْهُمَا كَمَا رَبَّيَانِي صَغِيراً"

> "Your Lord has decreed that you worship none but Him, and that you be kind to your parents. If one or both of them attain old age in their life, do not say to them a word of disrespect, nor repel them, but address them in terms of honour. And out of kindness, lower to them the wing of humility, and say, 'My Lord! Bestow on them Your mercy, just as they cherished me in childhood.'"[34]

---

34. (Q17, V23-24)

Also in *Surah al-Baqarah*, verse 83, Allah *SWT* says:

"وَإِذْ أَخَذْنَا مِيثَاقَ بَنِي إِسْرَائِيلَ لاَ تَعْبُدُونَ إِلاَّ اللّهَ وَبِالْوَالِدَيْنِ إِحْسَاناً وَذِي الْقُرْبَى وَالْيَتَامَى وَالْمَسَاكِينِ وَقُولُواْ لِلنَّاسِ حُسْناً وَأَقِيمُواْ الصَّلاَةَ وَآتُواْ الزَّكَاةَ ثُمَّ تَوَلَّيْتُمْ إِلاَّ قَلِيلاً مِّنكُمْ وَأَنتُم مِّعْرِضُونَ"

> "And remember, We took a covenant from the children of Israel (to this effect): worship none but Allah; treat with kindness your parents and kindred, orphans and those in need; speak fair to the people; be steadfast in prayer; and give *zakah*."[35]

Children need to see respect demonstrated to parents and other elders in their everyday lives. North American culture makes it very difficult for children to learn this value without a genuine effort, consistent guidance and continuous training from their parents. In this society, children always hear comments such as, "Why not?", "It's not fair," and "I don't care" from their peers as well as from other adults. These types of comments and behaviours do not promote respect. They are based on the individualistic attitude of North America. These comments are self-centred and are only concerned with what the individual wants, without considering anyone else. Also, it is becoming very normal for children to make faces while they are talking to their parents at home, or to their teachers in school. This attitude is becoming such a habit for some children that most of the time they do not even think that they are making faces. This is another form of disrespect that should not be tolerated if you want your child to be a well-behaved Muslim child.

Parents must work hard to make sure that their children understand what is respectful and what is not. Parents can easily teach this by always treating each other with respect, so the children

35. (Q2, V83)

have a living example. Parents can also teach respect by treating their children in a respectful way, and by consistently instructing, training and demanding that the children do respectful things. For example, if they make faces while talking to you, remind them that they are making faces, and say to them, "Look at me. Am I making faces while I'm talking to you? Please don't make faces when you talk to me." Another example is to teach them to say "please" whenever they are asking for something, and "thank you" whenever something is given to them. Even something as simple as thanking their mother for the food on the dinner table gives them an idea of how much their parents do for them.

Even when disagreeing, the children should be taught to do it with respect. For instance, the parents take the children to the park to play. When it is time to go, the children ask, "Can we stay longer?" After the parents explain that it is time to go, the children insist that they still want to play. They begin to say, "It's not fair. Why do we have to go?" The parents should not tolerate this. If the children see that this disrespectful attitude is accepted, they will continue to behave this way. Parents can let the children ask **politely** to stay longer, but they should remember to say "please," and should know where the limit is and when to stop asking.

Following the **Indicate, Educate, and Train** technique is of great help in correcting such behaviour, as discussed at the end of the Self-Search chapter.

CHAPTER 6

ENCOURAGE AND EMPHASIZE POSITIVE ACTIONS

Without a doubt, Islam is a practical religion. As such, Islamic injunctions are within the capabilities of those who believe. This fact is clearly indicated in *Surah al-Baqarah*, where Allah *SWT* says:

"لاَ يُكَلِّفُ اللّهُ نَفْساً إِلاَّ وُسْعَهَا"

"Allah does not burden any soul beyond its capability."[36]

This concept is further emphasized by the *hadith* of the Prophet *SAAW*, which says:

"فإذا نهيتكم عن شيء فاجتنبوه، وإذا أمرتكم بأمر فأتوا منه ما استطعتم"

"Whatever I order you to do, do it as best as you can. And whatever I forbid you to do, avoid it completely."[37]

It is very clear from this that Allah *SWT* does not burden any soul with more than it can handle, and that the Prophet *SAAW* advised us to make things easy for people, not difficult. In addition, encouraging and emphasizing positive actions was always part of the Prophet's *SAAW* methodology in helping Muslims fulfill their religious commitment and elevate their level of *iman* and Islamic practices.

---

36. (Q2, V286)
37. Agreed Upon

It was reported by Talhah Ibn Ubaid-Allah that a man from the Arab people came to the Prophet *SAAW* and said, "O Prophet of Allah, tell me what Allah has ordered me to do in terms of prayer." The Prophet *SAAW* said, "The five daily prayers, unless you want to volunteer more."

The man said, "O Prophet of Allah, tell me what Allah has ordered me to do in terms of fasting." The Prophet *SAAW* said, "The month of Ramadan, unless you want to volunteer more."

The man said, "O prophet of Allah, tell me what Allah has ordered me to do in terms of *zakah*." The Prophet *SAAW* told him.

The man then said, "By Allah Who honored you with the Truth, I am not going to do any more or any less than what Allah has ordered me to do." The Prophet *SAAW* said, "This man will achieve prosperity if he does what he said he will do."

This shows how the Prophet *SAAW* emphasized the positive aspect of what the man said, and encouraged him. He did not ask him to do more, simply because, if someone starts to practice acts of worship in the proper way, eventually she will find the beauty and sweetness of it and will do more on her own. However, if the Prophet *SAAW* had asked the man to do more, he may have felt that it was too much and might not have started to practice at all.

It is important for parents to observe this principle during the *tarbiyah* process with their children. Parents should only ask children to do what they are able to do, and they should praise them for their achievements.This will encourage them to do more. Encouragement is a great motivator that ensures high self-esteem, self-confidence, and helps the child to be ready for new challenges.

Continue to encourage your child; for **example**, if he spends some time colouring a picture, your response should be, "*Masha'Allah*, you spent all this time colouring this nice picture. What a great effort, my dear." Even if the colours were not the best ones for the picture or the child did not colour within the lines, do not emphasize this. Instead, you should emphasize the effort that your child made in colouring the picture. Emphasizing children's shortcomings has been proven to discourage them from trying the same type of activity again. As parents, you do not want to discourage your child and end up with such results.

Another common example of discouraging the child often occurs in parents' responses and comments to the child during prayer training. Usually, parents ask the child to stay in the same line with them during the *jama'a* prayer. Of course, a young child's attention span is very short and it is very difficult for her to stand still for a long time. Therefore, she will naturally move during the prayer. The big mistake that some parents make is that, as soon as the prayer finishes, they reprimand the child by saying, "How many times have I told you not to move during the prayer?" This is a discouraging comment. Such a comment is emphasizing the child's negative action. Instead, the parent should say, "*Masha'Allah*, you were able to stand still during the whole first rak'ah of the prayer. This is good. *Insha'Allah* next time you can do two *rak'ah*."

CHAPTER 6

DO THINGS STEP BY STEP AND CONSIDER THE LEVEL OF THE CHILD

The concept of doing things gradually, or step by step, when raising children is a basic principle of their training and development that parents must be sure to implement. The *seerah* of the Prophet *SAAW* is full of examples supporting this concept, such as:

"عن أَبي مَعْبَدٍ عن ابنِ عباسٍ "أنّ رسولَ الله صلى الله عليه وسلم بَعَثَ مُعَاذاً إلى اليَمَنِ فقال له: إنّكَ تَأْتي قَوْماً أَهْلَ كِتَابٍ فادْعُهُمْ إلى شَهَادَةِ أَنْ لا إلهَ إلاّ الله وأَنّى رَسُولُ الله، فإنْ هُمْ أَطَاعُوا لِذَلِكَ فأَعْلِمْهُم أن الله افترَضَ عَلَيْهِم خَمْسَ صَلَوَاتٍ في اليَوْمِ واللّيْلَةِ، فإن هُمْ أَطَاعُوا لِذلكَ فأَعْلِمْهُمْ أنّ الله افْتَرَضَ عَلَيْهِم صَدَقَةً في أَمْوَالِهِمْ تُؤْخَذُ مِنْ أَغنيَائِهِمْ وتُرَدّ على فُقَرائِهِمْ، فإنْ هُمْ أَطَاعُوا لِذَلكَ فإيّاكَ وكَرَائِمَ أَمْوَالِهِمْ. واتّقِ دَعْوَةَ المَظْلُومِ فإنّهَا لَيْسَ بَيْنَهَا وبَيْنَ الله حِجَابٌ"

"It was narrated by Abu Ma'bad that when the Prophet *SAAW* sent Mo'az Ibn Jabal *RAA* to Yemen, he *SAAW* told him, 'You are going to the people of the book. The first thing you should do is invite them to bear witness that there is no deity but Allah and that Muhammad is His messenger.' Then he said, 'If they accept this from you, then tell them that Allah makes it obligatory for them to pray five times a day. If they accept this, tell them that Allah orders that a charity must be taken from their rich and given to the poor. If they accept this, do not touch their lawful money and beware that there is no barrier between the prayer of the wronged and Allah.'"[38]

---

38. Tirmidhi

In this *hadith*, the Prophet *SAAW* establishes the importance of acting gradually and gently when introducing new concepts to people. This principle was also clearly demonstrated when drinking alcoholic beverages was prohibited. It was done gradually in three or four stages in the Qur'an before it became completely *haram*. First, the Qur'an hinted to the fact that things that make people drunk are not good, in *Surah al-Nahl*:

"وَمِن ثَمَرَاتِ النَّخِيلِ وَالأَعْنَابِ تَتَّخِذُونَ مِنْهُ سَكَراً وَرِزْقاً حَسَناً إِنَّ فِي ذَلِكَ لآيَةً لِّقَوْمٍ يَعْقِلُونَ"

"And from the fruits of date-palms and grapes you derive intoxicants as well as wholesome sustenance and provisions."[39]

The second stage is indicated in *Surah al-Baqarah:*

"يَسْأَلُونَكَ عَنِ الْخَمْرِ وَالْمَيْسِرِ قُلْ فِيهِمَا إِثْمٌ كَبِيرٌ وَمَنَافِعُ لِلنَّاسِ وَإِثْمُهُمَا أَكْبَرُ مِن نَّفْعِهِمَا"

"They will ask you [the Prophet *SAAW*] about intoxicants and games of chance. Say, 'In both there is great evil as well as some benefit for man; but the evil that they cause is greater than the benefit that they bring.'"[40]

Here, Allah *SWT* is indicating that the harm of drinking is much greater than the benefit.

The third stage came in *Surah al-Nisaa'*, when Allah *SWT* said:

"يَا أَيُّهَا الَّذِينَ آمَنُواْ لاَ تَقْرَبُواْ الصَّلاَةَ وَأَنتُمْ سُكَارَى حَتَّىَ تَعْلَمُواْ مَا تَقُولُونَ"

39. (Q16, V67)
40. (Q2, V219)

"O you who believe, do not attempt to pray while you are in a state of drunkenness, (but wait) until you know what you are saying."[41]

The final stage was in *Surah al-Ma'idah,* when Allah *SWT* said:

"يَا أَيُّهَا الَّذِينَ آمَنُواْ إِنَّمَا الْخَمْرُ وَالْمَيْسِرُ وَالأَنصَابُ وَالأَزْلاَمُ رِجْسٌ مِّنْ عَمَلِ الشَّيْطَانِ فَاجْتَنِبُوهُ لَعَلَّكُمْ تُفْلِحُونَ"

"O you who believe, intoxicants, gambling, idolatrous practices, and fortune telling are a loathsome evil of Satan's doing. Therefore, shun them so that you might attain to a happy state!"[42]

Each stage played an important role in preparing the believers to accept the final prohibition, by considering that it is human nature to hold on to old habits. It took a few years to change this unacceptable social behaviour.

Parents should also be gradual when trying to change any of their children's behaviours. Do not expect miracles; behavioural change does not come easily. It takes time and requires persistence, repetition, and gradual gains.

For example, a teenager might be used to going to bed every night at 11:00 p.m. This is a bad habit that his parents should change because he needs enough sleep during the night to be fully responsive and active during the day and to pay good attention to his lessons at school. To change this habit, parents cannot force him to go to bed at 8:00 p.m. at once; this would be very difficult to implement. Instead, they should apply the concept of gradual change by first asking the teen to go to bed at 10:30, and continue doing this for a week. Then, they can set another time, such as 10:00 p.m., for the following week, and so on until they reach their target of 8:00 p.m.

---

41. (Q4, V43)
42. (Q5, V90)

CHAPTER 8

COMMUNICATE CLEARLY AND EFFECTIVELY

The Prophet *SAAW* was the most effective communicator. He used various techniques to express his views and ideas in the most effective way. The following *ahadith* illustrate some of these techniques.

• "It was reported on the authority of 'A'isha *RAA* that the Messenger of Allah *SAAW* **spoke clearly and plainly** so that everyone who listened to him would understand him."[43]

• Also, "it was reported by Anas *RAA* that the Messenger of Allah *SAAW* **used to repeat his words three times** so that their meaning would be fully understood."[44]

• When the Prophet *SAAW* wanted to deliver a message to someone, he would attract their attention in various ways, such as:

– *By starting with a question*:

"It was reported that the Prophet *SAAW* said:

"أتدرون من المفلس"

'Do you know who is a bankrupt person?'"[45]

"Also during the Farewell *Hajj*, he started his speech by asking the congregation, 'Do you know which day this is? Do you know which month this is? Do you know which year this is?'"

---

43. Abu Dawud

44. Bukhari

45. Tirmidhi

– *By giving examples:*

It was reported that the Prophet *SAAW* said, that "The believers, in their mutual kindness, compassion, and sympathy, are like a body. If one of the organs is afflicted, the whole body responds to it with wakefulness and fever."[46]

He also said, "You and I are like the man who lit a fire that moths and other insects started running toward and falling into, and who was trying to stop them. I am like this man, trying to hold you by your waists (to save you) from Hell, but you are escaping from my hands."[47]

He also said, "The five prayers are like a river that passes by the gate of your home, in which you take a bath five times daily."[48]

– *By using reason and logic* to explain his argument in a convincing way, to touch the person he was talking to. The following is an example from the Prophet's *SAAW* teachings:

حدثنا عبد الله حدثني أبي حدثنا يزيد بن هارون حدثنا جرير حدثنا سليم بن عامر عن أبي أمامة قال:– إن فتى شابا أتى النبي صلى الله عليه وسلم فقال: يا رسول الله ائذن لي بالزنا فأقبل القوم عليه فزجروه وقالوا: مه مه فقال: ادنه فدنا منه قريبا قال: فجلس قال: أتحبه لأمك قال: لا والله جعلني الله فداءك قال: ولا الناس يحبونه لأمهاتهم قال: أفتحبه لابنتك قال: لا والله يا رسول الله جعلني الله فداءك قال: ولا الناس يحبونه لبناتهم قال: أفتحبه لأختك قال: لا والله جعلني الله فداءك قال: ولا الناس يحبونه لأخواتهم قال: أفتحبه لعمتك قال: لا والله جعلني الله فداءك قال: ولا الناس يحبونه لعماتهم قال: أفتحبه لخالتك قال: ولا والله جعلني الله فداءك قال: ولا

46. Agreed upon
47. Muslim
48. Muslim

الناس يحبونه لخالاتهم قال: فوضع يده عليه وقال: اللهم اغفر ذنبه وطهر قلبه وحصن فرجه فلم يكن بعد ذلك الفتى يلتفت إلى شيء.

"It was reported that when a young man came to the Prophet *SAAW* asking for permission to fornicate, the Prophet *SAAW* asked him, 'Would you like it for your mother?' The man said, 'No.' The Prophet *SAAW* asked him, 'Would you like it for your sister?' The man replied, 'No.' The Prophet *SAAW* asked him, 'Would you like it for your aunt?' He replied, 'No.' The Prophet *SAAW* asked him, 'Would you like it for your cousin?' The man said, 'No.' Then, the Prophet *SAAW* told him, 'Likewise, other people would also not like it for their female relatives.' And he put his hand on the young man's chest and prayed that Allah grant him chastity."[49]

The Prophet *SAAW* discussed the matter logically with the young man and gave him a clear explanation that touched him. This is an important principle to follow with everybody, especially with children. They deserve to be given a proper explanation that suites their level of understanding. Unfortunately, some parents do not use logic or do not explain things properly when their children ask certain questions. Some parents may not even allow their children to discuss or ask questions related to the *deen*. They might order their children to do something and only provide an explanation such as, "You have to do that because I said so!" or "You have to do it because you are a Muslim." Such explanations are not enough. Parents should not only *allow* their children to ask questions, but should even *encourage* them to do so, and then provide them with proper answers. This is the only healthy way to train our children to be strong Muslims and to be convinced about what they do. It will also provide them with proper answers that they can give to other people who may ask them why they behave in a certain manner or do certain things.

49. Ahmad

The result of effective and clear communication with children is long-lasting closeness and a strong bond between children and their parents. Certain times of the day are more effective than others for building these bonds. Among these special times are: **early morning**, as soon as the child wakes up; **after the child comes home from school; at the dinner table; and before the child goes to bed.** Parents should prepare themselves to make the most of these times and utilize them properly.

Early morning is the most suitable time to teach a child to memorize verses of the Qur'an and certain *du'as*, while he is getting ready for school. This is when child is fresh and well rested and when his mind is clear and more receptive to memorization. It is also a time to prepare your child for the day ahead of him, so he can start his day with the right attitude. Teaching your child the *du'a* for leaving the house is a strong asset for keeping him focused, guided, productive and positive about the tasks he has to fulfill during the day. Rather than telling our children, "Go, have fun," when they leave home in the morning, as North American culture promotes, we send them off with this beautiful *du'a*:

"باسْمِ اللَّهِ تَوَكَّلْتُ على اللَّهِ، اللَّهُمَّ إني أَعُوذُ بِكَ أنْ أضِلَّ أَوْ أُضَلَّ، أوْ أزِلَّ أَوْ أُزَلَّ،
أَوْ أظْلِمَ أَوْ أُظْلَمَ، أوْ أجْهَلَ أَوْ يُجْهَلَ عليَّ"

"In the name of Allah. I put my trust in Allah. Oh Allah, I seek refuge in you not to misguide anybody or to be misguided; not to humiliate anybody or be humiliated; not to oppress anybody or be oppressed; and not to mistreat anybody or be mistreated."[50]

This is a wonderful *du'a*. If our children remember, understand and repeat this *du'a* every day when they leave home in the morning, they will always behave in a responsible way toward themselves and others.

---

50. Ibn Majah, Tirmidhi, Abu Dawud

After a child comes home from school is a great time to listen to her and hear how she did at school. It is a good time for her to share her feelings if she faced any problems during the school day. A major problem faced by many Muslim families living in North America is when both parents are working full time and are not at home when their child returns from school. The child gets frustrated because her parents are not there for her to discuss her feelings with them and get some guidance regarding her pressing needs. In these cases, the child usually ends up discussing her problems with her peers, and usually receives the wrong advice.

At the dinner table is the time for the whole family to speak about their day. Dad or Mom might start and the children follow.

Bedtime is storytime. Mom and Dad should take turns telling stories for children before they go to bed. Stories of the life of the Prophet *SAAW*, of his companions, of the prophets in general, and of Muslim heroes are the most suitable type of stories for children to hear before going to sleep. Other stories that deal with certain problems can also be told.

The effectiveness of the above times depends on the child's age. While the morning and bedtime is more effective for young children and children in their early school years, right after school and at dinner time are much more effective for teenagers and children in their middle-school years.

Keeping an open channel of communication with the child when he is young is an important investment for the teenage years. The nature and type of communication will vary according to the child's age and needs. For a baby or infant, kissing, hugging, and tickling are good means of communication. For a toddler, storytelling at bedtime, songs, and family games provide further ways of communication. In later years, going to the park with the child and playing a ball game is a very effective form of communication. In such a setting, the child will feel more at ease and will talk to her parents about any concerns that she may have. All these ways of communicating help to establish a strong bond between children and their parents and enhance their relationship and level of mutual respect.

CHAPTER 9

ALLOW CHILDREN TO EXPRESS THEIR FEELINGS AND SHARE THEIR HAPPINESS AND PAIN

Allowing children to express their feelings and share their happiness and pain is a very important principle in children's *tarbiyah.* If parents successfully allow children to express their feelings, the children will always come back to them, seeking their help with any problem. When parents do not allow children to express their feelings, the children will keep things to themselves and will not disclose any information to them. This is a serious mistake that many parents make. It creates a communication gap between children and parents. Children need to express their feelings to their parents, otherwise they will find somebody else to talk to, such as a teacher, counselor, friend, or even one of their peers, who could mislead them. This could also be the beginning of keeping all their emotions from their parents, which can lead to a serious problem: that the children do not listen to their parents or consult with them when they have a problem or issue to discuss. The Prophet *SAAW* allowed young children to express their feelings and did not deny them such expression. Actually, he even acknowledged these feelings and shared in them with the children. It was reported that one day, the Prophet *SAAW* came to the house of Abu Bakr *RAA* and found 'A'isha *RAA* behind the door crying. He asked her why and she complained about her mother. The Prophet *SAAW* cried in sympathy for her and talked to her mother to solve the problem. This shows how the Prophet *SAAW* shared the feelings of 'A'isha *RAA*, who was only six years old at the time.

How can you apply such a principle with your children? Let us give you a simple **example** to illustrate. Suppose your child comes home from school one day in a bad mood, complaining that he had a problem with some of his peers. Some parents may directly respond to their child by saying, "This is not a problem. You are a big boy now and you shouldn't worry about these little things," without allowing the child to express his feelings. This is not the right approach to solve the problem. As a parent, you should try to use the Prophet's *SAAW* method. Ask the child to describe the problem for you and show sympathy for him. Tell him that you would have felt the same if such a thing had happened to you. Ask him if he wants you to intervene to help solve the problem. Suggest various ideas to deal with the problem and let him choose, with your guidance, the most suitable one. In this way, you have shared his feelings, helped him analyze the problem and guided him through the pros and cons of each suggested solution. This is a valuable exercise for your child. The time you spend with him is very well spent and he will appreciate your understanding and your being with him during difficult times. What he needed most was to feel your support and encouragement.

CHAPTER 10

ACTIVE LISTENING

Active listening is the attempt made by the listener to restate the feeling and/or content of what the speaker has said. It implies that the listener is trying to understand how it would feel to be the other person. It implies that the other person is important and worth giving your attention and time to.

You cannot fake active listening because it demands more than nodding your head and occasionally saying "uh-huh." Active listening is difficult because it means that you must try to understand another person's communication and not judge what they are saying. By withholding judgment, you are indicating to the other person that you respect her and that she does not run the risk of being put down. Active listening is also a way of showing empathy, and empathy builds trust.

The Prophet *SAAW* is a good example of an active listener, even with his enemies and those who disagreed with him.

As parents, active listening is a great quality that we should develop when dealing with our children. It will earn their trust and help strengthen our relationship with them.

First and foremost, learn to listen effectively. This means:

Listen not only to the verbal message but also pay close attention to the body language. Less than 20% of what is understood comes from the actual words that are used. We respond much more to the tone of voice, eye contact, facial expressions, body position, and so on. One way to discover the messages that you are sending to your family members is to record a video of the family spending time together in a natural environment, with everyone's permission, of course. Watching such a video tape can be very informative and helpful in observing others' body language as well as your own.

Reflect, which means you repeat back to your child what you think he was saying and feeling, without judging him or trying to solve the problem. Simply allow the child to elaborate.

Clarify. Find out whether you correctly understood what the child said or whether you misinterpreted it. Have you overlooked any important details?

Empathize by trying to put yourself in your child's position. This may help you recall a similar incident that you have experienced in the past. Tell your child that you understand and care about how she feels.

These four tools may be enough. Remember, the child's primary need is to communicate and be understood. But if the child asks for, and seems to want, help in dealing with a particular situation, then you may try to ***SOLVE THE PROBLEM*** by asking your child what he thinks might help and whether there is anything you can do for him. Again, be careful. Do not impose your own solution on him. Simply suggest it and let him make the choice.

This sort of effective listening will not only ensure that you really hear what your child is saying, but it will also indicate to her that you can accept and understand all the other things she has wanted to share. That is when the real communication begins and it is a great source of support for the child.

Of course, parents must use the proper level of language. It was reported that the Prophet *SAAW* was like a child when he talked to children, and like a youth when he talked to youth. He shared their interests with them and spoke to them in their language, at their level. 'Ali Ibn Abi Talib *RAA* also said:

"حدثوا الناس بما يعرفون، أتحبون أن يكذب اللّه ورسوله"

We should "talk to people according to their level of understanding. Would you like them to deny the sayings of Allah *SWT* and his Messenger *SAAW*?"

Parents must also share activities with their children. This is important for their development. Sharing activities also opens up channels of communication and makes the children feel comfortable talking to their parents.

Example

Active listening requires the listener to give his undivided attention to the speaker. It is called active, and not passive, listening because the listener is actively involved in the conversation by doing such things as nodding his head, leaning forward and making eye contact with the speaker. Imagine how the child feels in the following scenario.

A young teenage boy has an issue at school one day, and comes home wanting to discuss it with his father. He walks through the front door and finds his father sitting on the couch, reading a magazine. "Good," the boy thinks to himself. "This is a perfect opportunity to tell him about what happened today." But as he greets his father and sits down next to him, his father does not take his eyes off the colourful pages of the magazine. "Dad?" he says. "Uh huh," the father replies with his eyes still glued to the magazine. "Um Dad, I wanted to tell you about something that happened to me at school today." The boy continues hoping that his father will soon realize that he wants him to focus on him, and not on the glossy paper in his hands. "Go ahead. I'm listening," the father replies, again without taking his eyes off the page he is reading for even a moment. But everyone knows that a person can't read a magazine and really listen to his son at the same time. This is also true with watching TV, talking on the phone and writing an e-mail. If parents do not show an interest when their children come to talk to them, then the children will not be interested in talking to their parents. In the case of this teenage boy, who has just been crushed by his father's apparent preference for a magazine over some quality time with his son, he may not turn to his father for advice about what happens in school anymore. Therefore, parents must be active listeners, not passive ones.

Chapter 11

Every Soul is Accountable for What it Earns

The concept of accountability is deeply entrenched in the Islamic system, in all fields and at all levels. It covers a very broad spectrum. Accountability is part of Islam's social, economic, political and moral system, and for a successful Muslim society, it must be practiced at the individual, family, community and societal levels. Therefore, parents have to understand this concept and learn how to use it effectively with their children for positive results *insha'Allah*. In *Surah Al-Muddaththir*, Allah *SWT* says:

"كُلُّ نَفْسٍ بِمَا كَسَبَتْ رَهِينَةٌ"

"Every soul is responsible for what it earns."[51]

In *Surah Al-Isra'*, Allah says:

"مَّنِ اهْتَدَى فَإِنَّمَا يَهْتَدي لِنَفْسِه وَمَن ضَلَّ فَإِنَّمَا يَضِلُّ عَلَيْهَا وَلاَ تَزِرُ وَازِرَةٌ وِزْرَ أُخْرَى وَمَا كُنَّا مُعَذِّبِينَ حَتَّى نَبْعَثَ رَسُولاً"

"Whoever chooses to follow the right path, follows it for his own good; and whoever goes astray, goes astray to his own detriment; and no bearer of burdens shall be made to bear another's burden."[52]

51. (Q74, V38)
52. (Q17, V15)

Also, in *Surah Al-Baqarah*, Allah says:

"لاَ يُكَلِّفُ اللّهُ نَفْسًا إِلاَّ وُسْعَهَا لَهَا مَا كَسَبَتْ وَعَلَيْهَا مَا اكْتَسَبَتْ"

"God does not burden any human being with more than he is well able to bear. In his favour shall be whatever good he does, and against him, whatever evil he does."[53]

In *Surah Al-Zalzalah*, Allah says:

"فَمَن يَعْمَلْ مِثْقَالَ ذَرَّةٍ خَيْرًا يَرَهُ * وَمَن يَعْمَلْ مِثْقَالَ ذَرَّةٍ شَرًّا يَرَهُ"

"So whoever does good equal to the weight of an atom will see it; and whoever does evil equal to the weight of an atom will see it."[54]

These verses establish the concept of accountability and represent one of the basic principles in dealing with children. Children should be held accountable for what they do. They should feel the weight of the consequences of their deeds and mistakes. If they are not held accountable and do not feel the burden of the consequences of their actions, they will repeat the same mistakes over and over. They will not know when to stop, or what to do and what not to do. Here is a practical **example** of how parents sometimes fail to apply this principle, possibly sending the wrong message to their children and causing them to continue repeating a negative behaviour.

Ahmad is in third grade. He rides the school bus every day to school. His bus stop is one block away from his house and the bus comes at 7:45 a.m., sharp. More often than not, Ahmad misses the bus because he does not like to wait for it and only leaves home in a rush at the last minute. When this happens, Ahmad's mom usually drives him to school. This type of behaviour from Mom

53. (Q2, V286)

54. (Q99, V7-8)

does not encourage or reinforce positive practices on Ahmad's part. Therefore, he will continue to behave in the same way since he has not felt the weight of the consequences of his actions.

You may ask, what is the solution in a case like this? The solution lies in Mom making sure that Ahmad feels the consequences of his actions. The approach she uses will depend on Ahmad's personality. If Ahmad is a good student and enjoys going to school, Mom will not drive him to school for one day. Yes, he is going to miss one day of school, but he will learn a good lesson of accountability, not only by missing school, which he loves, but also by having to do extra work to catch up for the day that he was absent. If Ahmad is an average student who thinks that staying home is a reward, rather than a punishment, Mom should think of another way for him to feel the consequences of his actions. Maybe she should drive him to school, but also deduct from his allowance the equivalent of a bus ticket, or ask him to do some extra house chores to compensate for his Mom's wasted time.

Another example is with Fatmah, who is in seventh grade. Fatmah's mom prepares a bag lunch for her every day. Fatmah almost always forgets her lunch bag at home as she rushes to catch the school bus. If Mom delivers the lunch bag to the school, Fatmah will not learn any lesson and may continue to repeat the same mistake. If Mom ignores the situation and leaves Fatmah without a lunch, she will learn the consequences of her actions.

In this example, however, parents should not use this approach with a very young child who would not be able to stay the whole day at school without lunch.

In addition, parents should only use this principle when the child's negative behaviour becomes a pattern, that is, when it is being repeated frequently. Parents should not use this technique the first time the child makes a particular mistake. They should allow some room for accommodation and give their child the chance to correct her mistakes.

Chapter 12

Good Deeds Erase Bad Ones

The principle of good deeds erasing bad ones is clearly indicated in the Qur'an, in *Surat Hud*:

"إِنَّ الْحَسَنَاتِ يُذْهِبْنَ السَّيِّئَاتِ"

"Verily, the good deeds remove those that are evil."[55]

In *Surah al-Ra'd,* the same principle is supported again when the Qur'an describes those who have good understanding (*ulo al-albab*). It states that such people:

"وَيَدْرَؤُونَ بِالْحَسَنَةِ السَّيِّئَةَ"

"...turn off evil with good."[56]

This concept opens the door for repentance and for correcting mistakes and bad deeds. This is also emphasized by the Prophet *SAAW* in the following *hadith*:

It was reported by Abi Zar Jondob ibn Jonadah that the Messenger of Allah *SAAW* said:

"اتق الله حيثما كنت وأتبع السيئة الحسنة تمحها وخالق الناس بخلق حسن"

"Have *taqwa* towards Allah *SWT* wherever you are, and follow a bad deed with a good deed, so that you may erase it, and deal with people in a good manner."[57]

55. (Q11, V114)
56. (Q13, V22)
57. Tirmidhi

Parents must keep this principle in mind when dealing with their children. They have to give their children the opportunity to correct their mistakes by doing extra good deeds. As soon as the children do an extra good deed, parents should not remind them of their previous mistakes, or keep mentioning their mistakes when they make new ones and are punished for them. As soon as the child is punished for his mistake, he should not be reminded of it repeatedly. A common negative parental behavior is to recall the past as soon as their children commit another mistake. Some of them may say, "Remember that time when you did that bad thing?" or "Remember when you behaved badly during your uncle's visit?" or "Remember when you didn't help your sister and were rude to her?" and so on. Nobody enjoys hearing an exhaustive list of all her life's mistakes in the midst of a petty unrelated argument. It is just not fair fighting. Some parents do this even though the child was already punished for her mistakes and already suffered the consequences of her bad behaviour. This sort of action from the parents lowers the child's self-esteem and makes her feel that the parents are picking on her. This is not what we want for our children. We are aspiring to make them strong and confident Muslims. We must not be picky or fussy with them, especially if they have already performed good deeds to make up for their bad deeds. This is how we can practice this wonderful principle with our children, and together with the previous principle of accountability, we can help our children be better and stronger Muslims.

CHAPTER 13

FOLLOW UP ON ORDERS AND BE CONSISTENT

Various Qura'nic commandments came more than just once; they were repeated and emphasized in various ways. This indicates the importance of following up and being consistent. Furthermore, we read in the Qur'an, in *Surah Ta-Ha*:

"وَأْمُرْ أَهْلَكَ بِالصَّلَاةِ وَاصْطَبِرْ عَلَيْهَا ..."

"And enjoin prayer on your family, and be constant in offering it."[58]

This great verse establishes the importance of continuous and regular follow-up by parents when they instruct their children to do certain things or fulfill religious duties. It also emphasizes being patient during the process of training and coaching children, to ensure that the required results are achieved. The word *wastaber* in Arabic, as used in the above verse, is not only taken from the root word *sabr*, which means patience, but is also expressed with very strong emphasis. This means that parents should never give up. They should try every possible means of training their children to do the right thing and adhere to Islamic values. If one method of training does not work, they have to think of other methods and keep trying, without giving up.

Remember that the methods used by parents should suit their children's age. For **example**, with younger children, storytelling in a casual, informal, and warm atmosphere is very appropriate for teaching them certain values and moral characteristics. Parents must then follow up with the children on the characteristic they have just learned from the story; otherwise, the children may not implement what they have learned.

58. (Q20, V132)

The following is a **practical example** to illustrate this. A child has just been taught about the characteristic of respecting others. If parents notice that their child is behaving in a disrespectful way toward adults, such as talking to her father in a sharp or rude tone, or using unacceptable expressions like, "I don't care," what should the parents do? They should follow up using these steps:

• Firstly, whoever is dealing with the situation should try not to react directly to the child's behaviour. The parent should keep quiet for a while, try to control his anger and remain calm. Never react out of anger.

• Secondly, he should call his child to a private area of the house and speak to her in a firm and assertive, but not angry, tone. He should explain to her that the way she behaved was improper. All of this should be done in a polite and respectful manner, and the parent should point this out to his child. He might even ask the child, "Am I speaking to you in a rude way right now? No. I'm speaking to you calmly and respectfully." He should also remind his child of the saying of the Prophet Muhammad *SAAW:* "The one who does not have mercy on our young ones and does not show respect to our elders is not from among us."[59] The parent should ask his child to ask for Allah's forgiveness for her sin. Then, he should tell her to please repeat her action, but this time in a proper way, without being disrespectful, and without using unacceptable expressions or a rude tone of voice.

• Thirdly, when the child does as she is told, her parent should thank her and remind her not to repeat the disrespectful behaviour, or there will be consequences.

• Fourthly, after the child changes her behaviour, the parents must not insult or humiliate her over the incident. They must also refrain from regularly reminding the child of her mistakes.

• Fifthly, if the same behaviour recurs, parents should repeat the process, and they may add certain disciplinary measures to follow

59. Tirmidhi

up on their promise that actions have certain consequences and bad behaviour cannot go unpunished. These disciplinary measures could include depriving the child of certain privileges, for example, not allowing her to visit her friend for a week, or not letting her go to the community picnic.

Parents should also use some tools to help themselves in the follow-up process. These could be follow-up charts, displayed in an agreed-upon location in the house (such as on the refrigerator), or written contracts.

Parents absolutely must observe the principle of following up and being consistent. We emphasize again that when parents instruct their child to do something, even something little, they must be serious and they should be sure to make eye contact with the child. If the child does not carry out the instruction, parents must repeat the instruction in a firm and serious voice, but never lose their temper or shout. If a parent says something once and the child does not do it, ignoring this behaviour has serious consequences. From then on, the child will always take the parent's instructions lightly. However, if the parent follows up, the child will understand that the parent means business, that it is not a joke, and the child will take it seriously.

This principle applies to every instruction. However, a clear **example** that comes to mind, which may fit such a situation, is teaching a child to put on his seat belt in the car. If the parent ignores enforcing it, the consequences can be deadly.

CHAPTER 14

FIND SUITABLE ALTERNATIVES

In this Western society, where certain destructive social habits and television can have a bad influence on children, Muslim parents have the responsibility of finding proper recreational alternatives to fill the lives of their children. The following is an incident from the *seerah* to confirm this:

قدم رسول الله – صلى الله عليه وسلم – المدينة، ولهم يومان يلعبون فيهما. فقال: "ما هذان اليومان؟" قالوا: يومان كنا نلعب فيهما في الجاهلية.فقال رسول الله – صلى الله عليه وسلم –: "إن الله قد أبدلكم بهما خيرا منهما: يوم الأضحى، ويوم الفطر"

"When the Prophet *SAAW* came to Medinah, he found that they had two days of celebration and feasts. He told them that Allah *SWT* has replaced these two days for them with two better days, the two '*Eids*: '*Eid ul-Adhha* and '*Eid ul-Fitr*."[60]

From this incident, we can see that, to change certain bad habits that the people had, the Prophet *SAAW* did not simply order them to stop these habits, but he found a better alternative for them to fill the void that would result from stopping the old habits.

The following is an **example** of how parents can use this principle with their children.

There is no doubt that most of us would like to minimize the number of hours our children spend watching television or surfing the Internet. To do this we have to provide a better alternative,

---

60. Muslim

such as Islamic videos. *Alhamdulillah*, nowadays, we can find many more good, high-quality Islamic videos than even a few years ago. Although parents should use these videos with their children, we would like them to follow these suggestions:

• Do not let the Islamic video become another passive watching activity for your children. Sit with them and make it an enjoyable learning experience for both of you, as well as an opportunity for bonding and discussion.

• Do not allow your children to keep watching the same video repeatedly. It is better to provide alternatives that give them the chance to be active participants in activities such as:

– Going out together for hiking or bicycle trips
– Participating in community sports teams
– Going out for picnics
– Camping

We ask parents to make sure that the Islamic video that their children are watching is a legal copy. Parents must not copy videos from friends, or allow friends to copy their legally purchased videos. Besides being illegal, copying videos also has a negative impact on the financial well-being of Islamic-video producers, which can severely limit their ability to continue producing healthy, positive, and Islamic alternatives for our children.

Chapter 15

Use Examples from Their Environment

The Prophet *SAAW* taught us to always use examples from the immediate environment to make sure that the audience clearly understands what is meant. It was reported that the Prophet *SAAW* said:

"إن قامت الساعة وفي يد أحدكم فسيلة، فإن استطاع أن لا يقوم حتى يغرسها فليغرسها"

"If the Hour is to happen and one of you has a small plant in your hands and you are able to plant it, then plant it."[61]

It was also reported by Abu Musa Al-Ash'ari *RAA* that the Messenger of Allah *SAAW* said:

"مثل المؤمن الذي يقرأ القرآن كمثل الأترجة: ريحها طيب وطعمها طيب. ومثل المؤمن الذي لا يقرأ القرآن كمثل التمرة: لا ريح لها وطعمها حلو. ومثل المنافق الذي يقرأ القرآن كمثل الريحانة: ريحها طيب وطعمها مر. ومثل المنافق الذي لا يقرأ القرآن كمثل الحنظلة: ليس لها ريح وطعمها مر"

"A *believer* who recites the Holy Qur'an is like a **citron**, whose fragrance is sweet and whose taste is delicious. A believer who *does not* recite the Holy Qur'an is like a **date**, which has no fragrance but a sweet taste. A *hypocrite* who recites the Holy Qur'an is like the **colocynth**,[62] which is fragrant in scent but bitter in taste. The hypocrite *who does not* recite the Holy Qur'an is like **basil**, which has no fragrance and a bitter taste."[63]

---

61. Ahmad

62. *Colocynth*: a small bitter fruit that grows on a vine, also called *bitter apple*, found in the Mediterranean region.

63. Agreed upon

It was also reported on the authority of Ibn Omar *RAA* that the Messenger of Allah *SAAW* said:

"إِنَّمَا مَثَلُ صاحِبِ القُرآنِ كَمَثَلِ الإِبلِ المُعقَّلة إِنْ عاهَدَ عَلَيْها أَمْسَكَها، وَإِنْ أَطْلَقَها ذَهَبَتْ"

"The parable of the one who knows the Qur'an well is like the parable of the **camel** owner. If he watches over it, it will stay with him, and if he sets it free, it will go away."[64]

Sahl bin Sa'd *RAA* reported that the Messenger of Allah *SAAW* said to 'Ali *RAA*:

"فَوَاللّهِ لأَنْ يَهْدِيَ اللّهُ بِكَ رَجُلاً وَاحِداً خَيْرٌ لَكَ مِنْ حُمْرِ النَّعَمِ"

"By Allah, if a single person is guided by Allah through you, it will be better for you than if you owned a flock of **red camels.**"[65-66]

The above teachings of the Prophet *SAAW* show how, in his illustrations, he used fruits, vegetables, and animals that were well known to the common people of the Arabian Peninsula at the time. Using these elements of their immediate environment proved to be a very successful technique in clarifying the issue being discussed and in bringing the people closer together.

Likewise, parents should use examples from their children's environment when trying to teach them, so that they may relate to the discussion more easily. This is especially true with teenagers. In order to do this, however, parents have a great responsibility in terms of understanding the North American environment, knowing what it calls for, adopting what is good from it, and rejecting what is bad.

---

64. Agreed upon

65. A flock of red camels is an indication of wealth.

66. Agreed upon

The following are a few **examples** to illustrate this principle:

(a) One example that worked very well with our daughter was this discussion: "If you have a quiz to study for, how long in advance do you prepare? What if you have a test? Do you then prepare further in advance? What if you have an exam? Think of your life as the study period that you have before the most enormous exam you can imagine - the Day of Judgment. Don't you need to prepare for it?"

(b) A good analogy to use with your children when you are explaining why they should pay attention to their level of spirituality as much as they pay attention their material possessions is this: "When people in this society want to buy a stereo system, they call all the stores that sell stereos. Then they find out all the different prices of all the different models, and which is the best buy in terms of quality and price. Only when they are completely satisfied with the quality of the product do they buy it. But many of them do not pay attention to anything spiritual. They don't read their Holy book. They don't go to church. Look at how much these people care about their material belongings. Isn't your emotional and spiritual well-being more important than that? If a person had all the money in the world, she still couldn't buy peace of mind. But a person who is content with her life because it goes deeper than materialistic power will be happy even if she is poor or sick, because she knows that she will be going to a better place after this life.

CHAPTER 16

FAVORITISM IS NOT ALLOWED

Numan bin Bashir *RAA* reported that, "My father gave me a slave as a gift. He took me to Allah's Messenger *SAAW* so that he would witness it. The Messenger of Allah *SAAW* said, 'This gift that you have given to Numan, have you given such a gift to every son of yours?' He replied, 'No.' The Messenger of Allah *SAAW* said, 'Be mindful of your obligation to Allah and do justice to your children.' My father returned and took back his gift."[67]

Numan bin Bashir *RAA* also reported that the Messenger of Allah *SAAW* said:

"اعدلوا بين أولادكم، اعدلوا بين أبنائكم"

"Treat your children equally, treat your children equally, treat your children equally."[68]

It is very clear from this incident and this *hadith* that parents should not favour one child over another, especially in materialistic matters. This does not mean that parents have to buy exactly the same gift for each child, especially if the children are not within the same age range. Instead, it means that they should buy a different gift, but of similar value, or a gift that is acceptable to the child and suitable for his age.

Fairness is not only limited to gifts and the material aspects of life, but it also covers the emotional and psychological feelings of children. Parents should try their best to equally distribute the time they spend playing with their children and the attention they give to each of them, even the hugs and kisses. Here are some practical **examples and situations** to look out for in avoiding favoritism.

---

67. Agreed upon

68. Ahmad, Ibn Hibban, and Sunnan

• When going out, parents should take turns taking different children with them.

• Parents should make a point of attending their children's school functions and special events, such as school plays and sports tournaments, equally.

• Parents should cater the time they spend with each child to the activities and interests of that particular child. A parent should not assume, because her oldest son likes to play baseball, that her younger son would like to play baseball as well.

• If one child requires more help with her schoolwork, parents should not count this as part of the fun time they spend with her.

• Parents must not take sides with their favourite child in the case of a conflict. They must always look at the facts and use them to judge the situation. Parents who take sides or favour one child over the others only cause resentment between their children, which generates sibling rivalry.

When the Prophet *SAAW* sat in gatherings with his companions, he would leave each one of them with the impression that he was the most beloved person to the Prophet *SAAW*. This is an important lesson for parents, who should always try their best to leave the same impression on all of their children, even if their love for one child is more than for the others.

Chapter 17

Be Brief and Use Wisdom When Preaching

Allah *SWT* has said:

"ادْعُ إِلى سَبِيلِ رَبِّكَ بِالْحِكْمَةِ وَالْمَوْعِظَةِ الْحَسَنَةِ"

"Invite people to the way of your Lord with wisdom and kind advice."[69]

Using wisdom when inviting others to the path of Allah *SWT*, or when correcting someone's negative behaviour, is highly recommended because of the great impact it will have on their reaction. If wisdom is coupled with gentle and kind advice, the result is usually positive and people will respond favourably to the advice given. The Prophet *SAAW* always observed this principle when moulding the personalities of his companions and in correcting or rectifying their mistakes. In addition, he never bored them with repeated instructions at times when repetition was unnecessary, nor was he harsh. The following two *ahadith* clearly illustrate this wonderful behaviour of the Prophet *SAAW*:

عن أبي وائل، قال: كان عبدالله يذكرنا كل يوم خميس. فقال له رجل: يا أبا عبدالرحمن! إنا نحب حديثك ونشتهيه. ولوددنا أنك حدثتنا كل يوم. فقال: ما يمنعني أن أحدثكم إلا كراهية أن أملكم. إن رسول الله صلى الله عليه وسلم كان يتخولنا بالموعظة في الأيام. كراهية السآمة علينا.

69. (Q16, V125)

"Abi Wa'il Shaqiq bin Salama *RAA* reported that Ibn Mas'ud *RAA* used to preach every Thursday. A man said to him, 'Abu Abdul-Rahman, we like your speeches, and we would like you to deliver us a lecture every day.' He replied, 'There is nothing to keep me from preaching and giving you a lecture every day, but I am afraid of boring you. I follow the same method in preaching to you that the Messenger of Allah *SAAW* used when preaching to us, out of fear of boring us.'"[70]

Here is another *hadith* that illustrates the same concept:

عن مُعَاوِيَةَ بنِ الْحَكَمِ السّلَمِيّ قال: صَلّيْتُ مَعَ رسولِ الله صلى الله عليه وسلم فَعَطَسَ رَجُلٌ مِنَ الْقَوْمِ، فَقُلْتُ: يَرْحَمُكَ الله، فَرَمَانِي الْقَوْمُ بِأَبْصَارِهِمْ، فَقُلْتُ: وَاثُكْلَ أُمّيَاهُ، مَا شَأْنُكُم تَنْظُرونَ إِلَيّ. قال: فَجَعَلُوا يَضْرِبُونَ بِأَيْدِيهِمْ عَلَى أَفْخَاذِهِمْ فَعَرَفْتُ أَنّهُمْ يُصَمّتُونِي. قال عُثْمَانُ: فَلَمّا رَأَيْتُهُمْ يُسكّتُونِي لَكِنّي سكَتّ. فَلَمّا صَلّى رسولُ الله صلى الله عليه وسلم بِأَبِي وَأُمّي مَا ضَرَبَنِي وَلا كَهَرَنِي وَلا سَبّنِي، ثُمّ قال: إنّ هَذِهِ الصّلاَةَ لا يَحِلّ فيها شَيْءٌ مِنْ كَلامِ النّاسِ هَذَا إِنّمَا هُوَ التّسْبِيحُ وَالتّكْبِيرُ وَقِرَاءَةُ الْقُرْآنِ

Mu'awiya bin Al-Hakam As-Sulami *RAA* also reported, "While I was praying with the Messenger of Allah *SAAW*, a man in the congregation sneezed and I responded with, 'Allah have mercy on you.' The people stared at me with disapproving looks. So I said, 'May my mother bereave me![71] Why are you staring at me?' Thereupon they began to strike their hands on their thighs. When I saw them urging me to remain silent, I became angry but restrained myself.

70. Agreed upon

71. *Wa thukla umayah*. An Arabic expression meaning that it is better for a person to die and let his mother mourn his death than to repeat such a serious mistake.

When the Messenger of Allah *SAAW* concluded his prayer (I declare that neither before him nor after him have I seen a leader who gave better instruction than him, for whom I may give my father and mother as ransom), he neither argued with me nor beat me, nor reprimanded me. He said, 'Talking is not allowed during the prayer because prayer consists of glorifying Allah, declaring His greatness and reciting the Qur'an or words to that effect.'"[72]

It is of utmost importance that parents observe this principle of being wise and kind when they want to direct or correct their children's behaviour. Many parents nag their children frequently and on a regular basis. They boss them around at every opportunity, and instruct them to do various things. Some parents may even order them in a harsh and unpleasant way to do things that may not be within their capability, or do this in front of their peers. When parents preach and remind, they should do so only occasionally, but always in a gentle and kind manner, taking into consideration the child's age, level of understanding, and ability to act.

In the case of prayer, which is the most important ritual for a Muslim, the Prophet *SAAW* instructed us to provide our children with at least three years of training on how to perform it before inflicting any kind of punishment on them. This is a good lesson for us. Other matters that are less important than prayer may require even more training time.

72. Muslim

Chapter 18

Help the Child to be Capable and to Develop Skills

Parents are responsible for teaching their children the proper survival skills that are suitable for their environment and time. Islam encourages us to teach our children swimming, shooting, and horseback riding. It was narrated that the Prophet *SAAW* said:

"كل شيء ليس من ذكر الله عز وجل فهو لهو أو سهو، إلا أربع خصال: مشي الرجل بين الغرضين، وتأديبه فرسه وملاعبته أهله، وتعليم السباحة"

> "Every activity other than Allah's remembrance is considered a waste of time except four activities: When a man is training for shooting, when a man is domesticating his horse, when a man is entertaining his family, and when a man is teaching his children to swim."[73]

It was also narrated in the authentic collection of Imam Muslim *RAA* that the Prophet *SAAW* recited the verse:

"وَأَعِدُّوا۟ لَهُم مَّا ٱسْتَطَعْتُم مِّن قُوَّةٍ"

> "And prepare against them the utmost force you can,"[74] then said, "Truly, power is in being a good shooter, truly power is in being a good shooter, truly power is in being a good shooter."[75]

---

73. Al-Tabarani
74. (Q8, V60)
75. Muslim

As narrated in the authentic collection of Imam Al-Bukhari *RAA*, he *SAAW* also encouraged his companions to be good shooters and used to tell them during their training, "Improve your shooting skills and I am with you."

The above skills were all considered very important survival skills for the environment of the early Muslims. Without such skills, they would have had great difficulty in surviving and in calling others to the Path of Allah *SWT*.

There is a great lesson for all parents in this. They have to teach their children and give them opportunities to acquire the survival skills necessary for their environment. We would be shortsighted if we limit our understanding of the Prophet's *SAAW* advice and teachings to the few skills mentioned above. We should teach our children every possible skill required for their survival in Western society, such as self defence, the ability to make choices, sports skills, administrative skills, computer skills, communication skills, and business skills, to name a few.

Let us elaborate on how we can we teach our children at least one of these skills: decision-making. Being able to make the right decision is a very important quality, because life is all about making the right choice. If we want our child to grow up with the ability to make decisions and choose the right alternative, we have to train them properly. First of all, such a process should start at a very early age.

For example, even though a parent may be in a hurry when dressing her three-year-old boy, instead of dressing him in any outfit, she could take two outfits out of the closet, put them on the bed and ask him, "Which of these outfits would you like to wear?" This way, she is letting him make his own choice.

A parent may ask his four-year-old daughter, "Would you like to have pasta and meatballs for dinner tonight, or would you rather have chicken and rice?"

A parent can ask her six-year-old child, "Where do you want to spend Saturday? Would you like to visit your friend, Hasan, or would you rather go to the park?"

A parent can give his eight-year-old daughter the following choice, "Do you want us to alternate reading the Qur'an together, or do you prefer to read while I listen to you?"

Teenagers should be involved in making decisions with parents in various matters related to family affairs and activities, such as a long trip to visit one of the Muslim countries, deciding on where you are going to spend the summer vacation, or moving to a new house.

Giving children these kinds of choices in simple matters that are related to their environment and suitable for their age will help them develop the ability to make decisions, which is a very important skill for everyone. When they grow up and become teenagers, if they are pressured by peers to smoke, for example, they will be able to make the right choice and say no because they already know how to choose between alternatives. They were already trained early in life to make decisions based on the right information.

A young child who is never given the chance to make her own choices will be very vulnerable to peer pressure and will most likely become a follower. She will try to fit in, and will have great difficulty in saying no to her peers with confidence and without feeling defeated.

Our duty as parents is to provide such training to ensure that our Muslim teens are strong, confident, and will not give in to the first peer pressure they face *insha'Allah*. Helping our children become capable and skilled Muslims is one of the most effective ways of ensuring their healthy development.

Chapter 19

Cosult with Your Child

The Qur'an tells us in *Surah al-Saffat* about the story of Prophet Ibraheem *AS* and his son, Isma'il *AS*:

"فَبَشَّرْنَاهُ بِغُلَامٍ حَلِيمٍ فَلَمَّا بَلَغَ مَعَهُ السَّعْيَ قَالَ يَا بُنَيَّ إِنِّي أَرَى فِي الْمَنَامِ أَنِّي أَذْبَحُكَ
فَانظُرْ مَاذَا تَرَى قَالَ يَا أَبَتِ افْعَلْ مَا تُؤْمَرُ سَتَجِدُنِي إِن شَاءَ اللَّهُ مِنَ الصَّابِرِينَ"

"So We gave him the good news of a forbearing son. Then, when his son was old enough to work with him, he said, 'O my son! I have seen in a dream that I am offering you in sacrifice to Allah. Now [tell me] what you think!' The son said, 'O my father! Do as you were commanded. You will find me, if Allah so wills, to be one of the steadfast.'"[76]

Although Prophet Ibraheem *AS* had received an order from Allah *SWT*, he still consulted with his son, Isma'il *AS*, before carrying out the order. This should serve as a great lesson for all parents. When a parent consults with his child, it makes the child feel that she is part of what is going on. It is much more effective than simply giving orders, because the consultation process in itself is a learning experience for the child. Through the process of consultation, the child will establish priorities and learn responsible decision-making skills that will help her throughout her life. Also, if the child has been consulted and has been given the opportunity to discuss the issue, she will have a stronger conviction about the decision she makes, and when she reaches an agreement with her parents, she will feel a greater sense of responsibility to fulfill her part of the agreement. Of course, the parents must always provide guidance, follow-up, and supervision, as well.

---

76. (Q37, V101-102)

The process of consulting the child can start at a very early age. All the **examples** described in the previous pages apply to this principle.

Another **example** is if a child wants to get involved in a specific program in the general community, as opposed to in the Muslim community. Before refusing to let a child participate, parents must stop and consider whether there is anything forbidden or wrong in the program. They should ask the child to research the pros and cons of the program and discuss them together. With the parents' guidance, the child should be able to make the right decision. For example, if he wants to get involved in sports or arts and there is a place where he can do this without compromising his Islamic principles, then why stop him from doing something he really wants to do? Parents may find that the program gives the child an opportunity to grow as a person and to learn how to interact, and find things in common, with people in the non-Muslim community. This skill will help children grow up to become teenagers who can make the right decision concerning more serious matters. Again, if they are offered a cigarette by one of their peers, they will be able to make the right decision and refuse such an offer, *insha'Allah.*

CHAPTER 20

ALWAYS KEEP A PROMISE

Keeping promises is one of the greatest virtues in Islam. The Qur'an emphasizes this fact in various verses, such as:

"يَا أَيُّهَا الَّذِينَ آمَنُواْ أَوْفُواْ بِالْعُقُودِ"

"O you who believe! Fulfill (all) obligations..."[77]

The Qur'an indicates that it is a sign of righteousness to fulfill contracts and keep promises. It says:

"وَالْمُوفُونَ بِعَهْدِهِمْ إِذَا عَاهَدُواْ"

"...and those who fulfill the contracts that they have made..."[78]

In *Surah Maryam* the Qur'an praises Prophet Isma'il *AS* for always fulfilling his promise:

"وَاذْكُرْ فِي الْكِتَابِ إِسْمَاعِيلَ إِنَّهُ كَانَ صَادِقَ الْوَعْدِ وَكَانَ رَسُولاً نَّبِيّاً"

"Also mention in the Book (the story of) Isma'il. Verily, he was true to what he promised, and he was a messenger (and) a prophet."[79]

In *Surah al-Mu'minun*, the Qur'an promises success and prosperity to those who keep their promises. It says:

---

77. (Q5, V1)
78. (Q2, V177)
79. (Q19, V54)

"وَالَّذِينَ هُمْ لِأَمَانَاتِهِمْ وَعَهْدِهِمْ رَاعُونَ"

"Those who faithfully observe their trusts and their covenants[shall inherit Paradise]."[80]

The teachings of the Prophet Muhammad *SAAW* are full of advice and illustrative examples related to keeping promises. Here is a very vivid example:

عن عَبْدِ الله بن عَامِرٍ أَنَّهُ قالَ: "دَعَتْنِي أُمِّي يَوْماً وَرَسُولُ الله صلى الله عليه وسلم قاعدٌ فِي بَيْتنا، فقالَتْ هَا تَعَالَ أُعْطِيكَ، فَقالَ لَهَا رَسُولُ الله صلى الله عليه وسلم وَمَا أَرَدْتِ أَنْ تُعْطِيه؟ قالَتْ أُعْطِيه تَمْراً، فقالَ لَهَا رَسُولُ الله صلى الله عليه وسلم: أَمَا إِنَّكِ لَوْ لَمْ تُعْطِهِ شَيْئاً كُتِبَتْ عَلَيْكِ كَذِبَةٌ".

Abd Allah Ibn Amer reported that: "My mother asked me to come to her with her hands closed, saying, 'If you come to me I'll give you such and such.' The Prophet *SAAW* was in our house. He *SAAW* asked her, 'What do you want to give him?' She replied, 'I will give him dates.' The Prophet *SAAW* told her, 'If you have nothing in your hand, it will be considered a lie on your part.'"[81]

From this *hadith*, we learn that before making a promise, we must first consider whether it is within our reach. For **example**, we must not promise a child something lavish or expensive if we know that it will be difficult for us to buy.

If parents make a promise to their child, trying their best to fulfill that promise will have a significant impact on the child's personality. Some parents use promises to get themselves out of certain situations, without thinking about the consequences or

80. (Q23, V8)

81. Abu Dawud

without intending to fulfill the promise. This is a huge mistake. Parents must only make promises that they can keep, and must not use promises as bribes.

For **example**, if a parent wants her children to memorize the Qur'an, she must explain why and convince them that it is important. She should not simply promise material things as a reward. Although there is nothing wrong with using gifts as encouragement, a more productive method is to promise them an hour of quality time in the park or a visit to a friend's house when they finish the task.

Another point to emphasize, which is related to making promises, is the light threats that some parents direct at their children to get out of certain situations or to keep them quiet. Sometimes, parents take these threats to the extreme without thinking about whether they can follow through with them. For **example**, if the family is driving on the highway and one of the children is making noise, a parent may say, "Hasan, if you don't stop making noise at once, I'll stop the car and leave you here on the side of the road!" No parent could ever follow through on such a threat. Therefore, the next time the parent gives an instruction, the child will not trust his parent or take him seriously because he failed to follow through on his threat, since it was irrational. Thus, making sure that parents use only rational threats that they can follow through with is very important.

Even if the punishment is rational, parents must not promise it unless they will definitely follow through with it. For **example**, a parent should not tell his child that she is grounded for a week if he only maintains the punishment for the first few days. Even if the parent intended to ground her for the whole week, the child will learn to belittle whatever punishment her parent threatens, because his follow-through was incomplete.

Chapter 21

Touch Their Soul and Awaken Their Conscience

In an authentic *hadith*, the Prophet *SAAW* said:

إنكم تختصمون إليّ وإنما أنا بشر ولعل بعضكم ألحن بحجته أو قد قال لحجته من بعض فأني أقضي بينكم على نحو ما أسمع فمن قضيت له من حق أخيه شيئا فلا يأخذه فإنما أقطع له قطعة من النار يأتي بها أسطاما في عنقه يوم القيامة

> "Two men came to the Prophet *SAAW* to resolve a dispute that occurred between them. The Prophet *SAAW* told them both, 'I am a human being like you and when you ask for my judgment on an issue, and perhaps one of you is more eloquent and expressive in presenting his case, I may judge in his favour because of this, although the right may be with his counterpart. If I do this, I am giving him a piece of the hellfire and he is free to take it or leave it.'"[82]

Upon hearing this, both companions started crying and both of them wanted to forfeit his right to the other. This is an example of how the Prophet *SAAW* awakened their consciences to the extent that they were even willing to sacrifice some of their rights to avoid being unjust or ending up with a piece of the hellfire.

The best way to touch the soul of your child or teen—or any human being for that matter—is to use the wonderful methodology of the Qur'an. The Qur'an is the word of the Creator, and the Creator knows His creation, what affects them most, and what touches their hearts and souls.

---

82. Agreed upon

"أَلَا يَعْلَمُ مَنْ خَلَقَ وَهُوَ اللَّطِيفُ الْخَبِيرُ"

"Should He not know what He created? And He is the Subtle, the Aware." [83]

Therefore, Qur'anic methodology tends to have a strong effect on people. The simplest, most direct and effective way of explaining a subject or of trying to influence and affect someone's views is to use the language and methodology of the Qur'an. For example, some people insist on talking about Islamic creed (*aqeeda*) or explaining the attributes of Allah *SWT* in a very technical and academic way, using dry expressions and confusing language. Neither the Qur'an nor the Prophet *SAAW* ever presented *aqeeda* or the attributes of Allah *SWT* in this way. For example, when the Qur'an talks about Allah's *SWT* attribute of being *al-Qaadir*, which translates as The One Who Has the Ability to do Anything, it touches the souls and the hearts of the readers by illustrating this attribute using a very interesting story, such as in *Surah al-Baqarah*:

"أَوْ كَالَّذِي مَرَّ عَلَى قَرْيَةٍ وَهِيَ خَاوِيَةٌ عَلَى عُرُوشِهَا قَالَ أَنَّى يُحْيِي هَٰذِهِ اللَّهُ بَعْدَ مَوْتِهَا فَأَمَاتَهُ اللَّهُ مِئَةَ عَامٍ ثُمَّ بَعَثَهُ قَالَ كَمْ لَبِثْتَ قَالَ لَبِثْتُ يَوْمًا أَوْ بَعْضَ يَوْمٍ قَالَ بَل لَّبِثْتَ مِئَةَ عَامٍ فَانظُرْ إِلَى طَعَامِكَ وَشَرَابِكَ لَمْ يَتَسَنَّهْ وَانظُرْ إِلَى حِمَارِكَ وَلِنَجْعَلَكَ آيَةً لِّلنَّاسِ وَانظُرْ إِلَى العِظَامِ كَيْفَ نُنشِزُهَا ثُمَّ نَكْسُوهَا لَحْمًا فَلَمَّا تَبَيَّنَ لَهُ قَالَ أَعْلَمُ أَنَّ اللَّهَ عَلَى كُلِّ شَيْءٍ قَدِيرٌ"

"Or like the one who passed by a village and it had tumbled over its roofs. He said, 'Oh! How will Allah ever bring it to life after its death?' So Allah caused him to die for a hundred years, then raised him up again. He said, 'How long did you remain (dead)?' The man replied, 'Perhaps I remained dead for a day or a part of a day.' He said, 'No.

You have remained (dead) for a hundred years. Look at your food and your drink, they show no change. And look at your donkey! And thus we have made of you a sign for the people. Look at the bones, how We bring them together and clothe them with flesh.' When this was clearly shown to him, he said, 'I now know that **Allah is Able to do all things.**"[84]

Other examples of Allah's *SWT* ability to do anything are in *Surah Maryam*, such as the story of Zakariya *AS*, and the story of the miraculous birth of 'Isa *AS*.[85]

When the Qur'an wants to illustrate Allah's *SWT* attribute of *al-Aleem*, which translates as The One Who Knows Everything, again it touches the hearts of readers with its eloquent language and wonderful presentation. For example, in *Surah al-An'am*, Allah *SWT* says:

"وَعِندَهُ مَفَاتِحُ الْغَيْبِ لاَ يَعْلَمُهَا إِلاَّ هُوَ وَيَعْلَمُ مَا فِي الْبَرِّ وَالْبَحْرِ وَمَا تَسْقُطُ مِن وَرَقَةٍ إِلاَّ يَعْلَمُهَا وَلاَ حَبَّةٍ فِي ظُلُمَاتِ الأَرْضِ وَلاَ رَطْبٍ وَلاَ يَابِسٍ إِلاَّ فِي كِتَابٍ مُّبِينٍ"

"And with Him are the keys of the *ghaib* (all that is hidden), none know them but He. And He knows whatever there is on the land and in the sea; not a leaf falls without Him knowing it. There is not a grain in the darkness of the earth, nor anything fresh or dry, that is not written in a clear record."[86]

Now, here is an **example** of how parents can use this method of touching the soul and awakening the conscience of our teenagers. During picnics or hiking trips, we should always try

84. (Q2, V259)
85. (Q19, V7-9 and V16-34)
86. (Q6, V59)

to allocate time to enjoy nature and observe the wonderful creation of Allah *SWT*, such as various kinds of trees, flowers, ants and bees. We should always make positive comments linking the scenic nature to Allah *SWT*, and praise Allah *SWT* for His wonderful creation. For example, if we observe the setting sun, instead of watching it silently, we can say, "*SubhanAllah*" or "*Masha'Allah,* this is just one of Allah's many creations." We can then recite the evening *athkaar* and encourage our children to do the same. This will soften their hearts and bring them closer to Allah's creation.

Chapter 22

Take Them on Trips that will Enhance Their Spirituality

The North American environment, with its materialistic focus, does not promote spiritual feelings or enhance closeness to Allah *SWT*. TV programs and the media contribute to low morality in North America. We should not measure our Islamic commitment and moral values against these norms. We should measure our moral values and religious commitment against the level of the *Sahaaba RAA* (the companions of the Prophet *SAAW*).

To make sure that this level is achieved, parents have to ensure a proper environment for their children to enhance their spiritual level. One way of achieving this is to provide spiritual trips for their children. These trips could be in the form of hiking trips, overnight trips to take in the beauty of the sky, stars, rivers, lakes, and trees and to enhance spiritual feelings. The Prophet *SAAW* instructed the *Sahaaba RAA* to say *Allahu Akbar* (Allah is Greatest) when they climbed a mountain and to say *SubhanAllah* (Glory be to Allah) when they walked in a valley. This is to link the beauty of nature to the power of Allah *SWT* and to enhance his Companions' level of belief (their *iman*). Therefore, parents must make sure to say these prayers and words of praise for Allah *SWT* whenever they arrange a trip for their children. North America has many wonderful nature trails and beautiful scenic routes that parents can drive through with their children to remember Allah *SWT*. For example, during the autumn season throughout the northern parts of North America, the leaves on the trees change colour and provide breathtaking scenery that makes everyone see the wonderful creation of Allah *SWT* and say, *SubhanaAllah*. Trips to watch this change of colour are a great source of spiritual enhancement for younger children.

Chapter 23

Do Not Accuse in a Direct Way

The Prophet *SAAW* taught us the etiquette of giving advice. The first and most important element of such etiquette is that the advice should be given in private, not in public. If we have to give the advice in public, we should not point fingers at the individual who made the mistake. Instead, we should give it in general terms, as the Prophet *SAAW* did. He used to climb the pulpit and say:

"مابال أقوام يقولون كذا وكذا"

"Why are certain people saying such and such?"[87]

Parents should observe this rule when they deal with their children's mistakes, especially if they have more than one child. Parents must not accuse or reprimand their child, especially in the presence of his friends or peers. Doing this will damage his self-esteem. It will also make him more defensive, which will not help in solving the problem at hand. Talking to the child in private, however, makes him much more receptive and gives him the chance to think about the actual situation rather than about the embarrassment he is feeling. In addition, the parents will find that they can be more objective in dealing with the child's mistake when they discuss it with him in private. It is an opportunity to tell him exactly what the mistake was, to educate him about why it was a mistake by quoting a verse from the Qur'an or one of the sayings of the Prophet *SAAW*, and to train him not to repeat the mistake.[88] The following is a practical **example** to illustrate this principle:

---

87. Nisa'i

88. Check the **Indicate, Educate, and Train** technique in earlier chapters of this book

A child is speaking to her parent or to an elderly person in a rude or disrespectful manner and is making faces while she is talking. This is unacceptable behaviour and the parent has to correct it. Rather than shouting or yelling at her in front of others, the parent should take her to another room and discuss the problem objectively with her. The parent should assume that the child did not know that her behaviour was unacceptable and should first indicate to her, in a calm but firm voice, that this behaviour is not acceptable. For example, the parent can say to the child, "Did you notice the way you were talking to me? Did you notice the tone of your voice and your facial expressions? Do you think this is a proper way to talk to others? Look at how I am talking right now. Am I talking rudely? Am I making faces at you? Do you think this is more respectful?" Most likely, the child may not even realize that she was being rude. This covers the **indication** step.

The next step is to **educate** her on why this behaviour is not acceptable. The parent should tell her either a verse from the Qur'an or one of the sayings of the Prophet *SAAW*. For example, the Prophet *SAAW* said:

"ليس منا من لم يرحم صغيرنا ويوقر كبيرنا"

> "The one who does not have mercy on our young ones and does not show respect to our elders is not from among us."[89]

Citing a verse or *hadith* will be more likely to convince her of the parent's point, because she will feel that the parent is not just inventing the rules but that they have a basis.

Finally, parents should not expect their child's behavior to change as soon as their mistake has been pointed out to them with an Islamic reference. Parents must **train** the child by repeating the process. They must also keep in mind that changing social behaviour requires time and follow-up.

89. Tirmidhi

Chapter 24

Choose the Lesser of Two Evils

Choosing the lesser of two evils is a great rule in Islamic jurisprudence that scholars deduced from the practices of the Prophet *SAAW* and the teachings of the Qur'an. This great rule should be understood properly and applied wisely by parents in North America. On the one hand, we have come across a great number of cases where parents have failed to use this rule and have ended up driving their children away from Islam. Some of those children have been lost completely to mainstream North American society, while others have lowered their Islamic commitment and practices to unacceptable levels.

On the other hand, we have also come across some parents who were wise enough to use this rule properly and, with the help of Allah *SWT*, ended up protecting their children from deviating from Islam. Most of these children are at a very good level of commitment to Islam and are now very strong, practicing Muslims. Let us illustrate what we mean with a few practical **examples**.

When it comes time for a young woman to wear a *hijab*, some parents insist that she wear long, loose dresses or skirts and a long *khimar* right away. While this is closer to the full *hijab*, it is often an extreme change for the young woman to make and she may not feel ready for it. Parents must remember that, at this age, teens are under tremendous peer pressure and are trying to fit in. They are seeking the approval of their peers and already feel different from their environment. We have come across cases where this has caused the young woman to completely reject the *hijab* and deviate from Islam. This is definitely **the greater harm**. Some parents see that the daughter does not feel ready to make a complete change, and allow her to start by wearing loose pants and loose, long-sleeved shirts with her headscarf. While this is the minimum for hijab and may not be considered by many as full *hijab*, it is better for the young woman to start off slowly and gradually make the change to looser clothing when she is ready. This way, we have avoided **the greater harm** of complete deviation from Islam by allowing **the lesser harm** of a temporary, lower level of *hijab*. While the young woman is in this first stage of wearing hijab, the parents should help her strengthen her belief by using various activities, such as spiritual nature trips, camps, and study circles, so that she may feel more ready to move on to the next level.

Our second **example** relates to memorizing the Qur'an. Some parents who want their children to memorize the Qur'an have very specific objectives regarding the amount to be memorized. For example, parents may set a goal such as requiring the child to memorize a certain number of *surahs* by the time he has reached a certain age. Parents may have even set an age for when they expect their child to have the whole Qur'an memorized. There is nothing wrong with setting targets for the child; however, if the child is very resistant to memorizing, or is constantly complaining that he is missing out on the fun that his peers are enjoying because he has to stay home to memorize, then he is at risk of hating the Qur'an. In this situation, the child is not likely to maintain a good relationship with the Qur'an when he is older and his parents no longer control his time. Some parents will not pay attention to this and will continue to push the child. This could lead the child to completely abandon the Qur'an and its teachings when he is older, because he only associates it with missing out on significant parts of his childhood. This is by far **the greater evil.**

Other parents may notice their child's resentment and make modifications to decrease the amount of Qur'an that he has to memorize, so that he does not feel overwhelmed or pressured. This is **the lesser evil**. Although the child will not have memorized as much, he will be more receptive to its meaning, and will maintain a good relationship with it. He will also be more likely to memorize more of it on his own, when he is older. This is consistent with the teachings of the Prophet *SAAW*, who said:

"فما أمرتكم به من شيء فأتوا منه ما استطعتم وما نهيتكم عنه فانتهوا"

"Do your best in what I have commanded you to do, and completely avoid what I have prohibited."[90]

In addition, Abdullah Ibn Mas'ud *RAA* said, "We used to memorize the Qur'an ten verses at a time. First, we would memorize the verses, then we would apply them. Then, we would move on to the next ten verses. This way, we learned knowledge as well as how to apply it."

This stresses the importance of applying what has been memorized of the Qur'an. Therefore, if the child in the above scenario has memorized the entire Qur'an but does not appreciate, understand, or apply it, nothing has been achieved.

We want to make it very clear that we are not discouraging Qur'anic memorization. Instead, we are pointing out that, just as with everything else, parents must be careful of how they approach it with their children and ensure that their method is not driving their children away from Islam.

90. Tabarani

Chapter 25

Utilize Opportunities

The story of Prophet Yusuf *AS* with his fellow inmates is a very clear illustration of the principle of utilizing opportunities:

"وَدَخَلَ مَعَهُ السِّجْنَ فَتَيَانَ قَالَ أَحَدُهُمَا إِنِّي أَرَانِي أَعْصِرُ خَمْراً وَقَالَ الآخَرُ إِنِّي أَرَانِي أَحْمِلُ فَوْقَ رَأْسِي خُبْزاً تَأْكُلُ الطَّيْرُ مِنْهُ نَبِّئْنَا بِتَأْوِيلِهِ إِنَّا نَرَاكَ مِنَ الْمُحْسِنِينَ * قَالَ لاَ يَأْتِيكُمَا طَعَامٌ تُرْزَقَانِهِ إِلاَّ نَبَّأْتُكُمَا بِتَأْوِيلِهِ قَبْلَ أَن يَأْتِيكُمَا ذَلِكُمَا مِمَّا عَلَّمَنِي رَبِّي إِنِّي تَرَكْتُ مِلَّةَ قَوْمٍ لاَّ يُؤْمِنُونَ بِاللّهِ وَهُم بِالآخِرَةِ هُمْ كَافِرُونَ * وَاتَّبَعْتُ مِلَّةَ آبَآئِـي إِبْرَاهِيمَ وَإِسْحَاقَ وَيَعْقُوبَ مَا كَانَ لَنَا أَن نُّشْرِكَ بِاللّهِ مِن شَيْءٍ ذَلِكَ مِن فَضْلِ اللّهِ عَلَيْنَا وَعَلَى النَّاسِ وَلَـكِنَّ أَكْثَرَ النَّاسِ لاَ يَشْكُرُونَ * يَا صَاحِبَيِ السِّجْنِ أَأَرْبَابٌ مُّتَفَرِّقُونَ خَيْرٌ أَمِ اللّهُ الْوَاحِدُ الْقَهَّارُ *مَا تَعْبُدُونَ مِن دُونِهِ إِلاَّ أَسْمَاء سَمَّيْتُمُوهَا أَنتُمْ وَآبَآؤُكُم مَّا أَنزَلَ اللّهُ بِهَا مِن سُلْطَانٍ إِنِ الْحُكْمُ إِلاَّ لِلّهِ أَمَرَ أَلاَّ تَعْبُدُواْ إِلاَّ إِيَّاهُ ذَلِكَ الدِّينُ الْقَيِّمُ وَلَـكِنَّ أَكْثَرَ النَّاسِ لاَ يَعْلَمُونَ * يَا صَاحِبَيِ السِّجْنِ أَمَّا أَحَدُكُمَا فَيَسْقِي رَبَّهُ خَمْراً وَأَمَّا الآخَرُ فَيُصْلَبُ فَتَأْكُلُ الطَّيْرُ مِن رَّأْسِهِ قُضِيَ الأَمْرُ الَّذِي فِيهِ تَسْتَفْتِيَانِ"

"And two young men entered the prison with him. One of them said, 'Verily, I saw myself (in a dream) pressing wine.' The other said, 'Verily I saw myself (in a dream) carrying bread on my head and the birds were eating from it.' (They said), 'Inform us of the interpretation of this. Verily, we think you are one of the good doers.' He replied, 'No food will come to you but I will inform you of it before it comes. This is what my Lord has taught me. Verily, I have abandoned the religion of people who do not believe in Allah, who are disbelievers in the hereafter, and I have followed the religion of my fathers, Ibraheem, Ishaq, and Ya'qub, and we could never attribute any partners whatsoever to Allah. This is from the grace of Allah to us and to mankind, but most men are ungrateful. O two companions of prison, are many lords (gods) better than Allah, the One, the Irresistible? You only worship names that you and your fathers have invented, names for which Allah has sent no authority. The command is for none but Allah. He has commanded that you worship none but Him. That is the true straight religion, but most men do not know. O two companions of prison, as for one of you, he will pour wine for his master to drink; and as for the other, he will be crucified and birds will eat from his head. Thus is the case judged concerning what you asked about.'"[91]

In this scenario, the Prophet Yusuf used the opportunity to make *da'wah* to his companions when they asked him to interpret their dreams. He did not answer their question immediately. Instead, he first talked to them about the issue that concerned him, the Oneness of Allah *SWT*. He had their attention and was able to deliver his message to them in the most effective way. He wanted to take advantage of the opportunity to guide his two fellow prisoners toward the true faith. Therefore, while promising that he would explain their dreams, he asked them to listen first to a short speech on the Oneness of God.

The following incident was reported by Jabir *RAA*:

أن رَسُول اللَّهِ صَلَّى اللَّهُ عَلَيهِ وَسَلَّم مر بالسوق والناس كَنَفَتَيْهِ، فمر بِجَدْيٍ أَسَكَّ مَيِّتٍ، فتناوله فأخذ بأذنه ثم قال: "أيكم يحب أن هذا له بدرهم؟" فقالوا: ما نحب أنه لنا بشيء وما نصنع به؟ قال: "أتحبون أنه لكم؟" قالوا: والله لو كان حياً كان عيباً أنه أَسَكّ فكيف وهو ميت! فقال: "فوالله للدنيا أهون على اللَّه من هذا عليكم"

91. (Q12, V36-41)

> "The Prophet Muhammad *SAAW* was walking with his companions and saw a dead sheep. He asked them, 'Who amongst you would buy this sheep with a *dirham*?' They replied, 'None of us.' The Prophet *SAAW* said, 'Likewise is the value of this worldly life; it is worth as little as this dead sheep.'"[92]

Here, the Prophet *SAAW* used the occasion to emphasize the fact that the value of this life is very little compared to the bounties prepared by Allah *SWT* in the hereafter. These bounties are for those who do righteous deeds and live this life according to the commands of Islam, to please Allah *SWT*.

The following are some **examples** to illustrate how parents can use this principle on different occasions.

1. A teen comes home from the school one day, upset because she received a lower score than she expected on one of her tests. She says, "I did my best. I even made lots of *du'a* to Allah *SWT* to help me get a good grade." This is an opportunity for her parent to explain the concept of *du'a* in Islam and to teach the teen that Allah *SWT* responds to it in different ways. Allah might grant a wish right away, or he might not grant it right away, but protect us from something harmful that was going to happen, or save it for us and give us more rewards in the hereafter. Parents can also use the occasion to help the teen understand that, in addition to making *du'a*, she has to work hard and do her best to achieve good grades.
2. When a loved one dies, or a close friend suffers a long time from an illness, this is an opportunity to talk to your child about the fact that life is a test and that we might all face these kinds of hardships. What matters is how we respond to them. We should do our best to alleviate our problems, and if we cannot, we should accept them, try to live with them, and help the sick person to cope with them.

---

92. Muslim

CHAPTER 26

ILLUSTRATE CONSEQUENCES IN A VIVID WAY

The Prophet *SAAW* used to illustrate the consequences of bad deeds in a very vivid way. He did this to get the attention of Muslims and emphasize how bad the deeds were so that they would not commit them. The following are some examples that illustrate this principle:

Ibn Abbas *RAA* reported that the Messenger of Allah *SAAW* said:

"مَثَلُ الَّذِي يَرْجِعُ فِي صَدَقَتِهِ كَمَثَلِ الْكَلْبِ يَرجِعُ فِي قَيْئِهِ فَيَأْكُلُهُ"

"A man who takes back his charity is like a dog who eats its own vomit"[93]

Nu'man Ibn Basheer *RAA* narrated that the Prophet *SAAW* said:

"مثل القائم على حدود الله والواقع فيها كمثل قوم استهموا على سفينة فأصاب بعضهم أعلاها وبعضهم أسفلها فكان الذين في أسفلها إذا استقوا من الماء مروا على من فوقهم فقالوا لو أنا خرقنا في نصيبنا خرقا و لم نؤذ من فوقنا فإن يتركوهم وما أرادوا هلكوا جميعا وإن أخذوا على أيديهم نجوا ونجوا جميعا"

"The likeness of the man who remains passive in the prescribed crimes of Allah and the man who commits them are like the people who boarded a ship after casting lots: some of them went to its lower deck and some to its upper deck. Those who are on its lower deck have to pass by those who are on the upper deck every time they want to bring water and thus they have troubled those on the upper deck.

93. Agreed upon

They say, 'If we dug a hole in our part of the ship (the bottom), we would not have to go to the upper deck every time we need water.' If those on the upper deck let them dig the hole, those on the lower deck would destroy everyone and also destroy themselves. If those on the upper deck prevented them from digging the hole, they would save everyone and save themselves."[94]

Ibn Abbas *RAA* reported the following:

أن رَسُولَ اللَّهِ صَلَّى اللَّهُ عَلَيْهِ وَسَلَّم رأى خاتماً من ذهب في يد رجل فنزعه فطرحه وقال: يعمد أحدكم إلى جمرة من نار فيجعلها في يده! فقيل للرجل بعد ما ذهب رَسُولِ اللَّهِ صَلَّى اللَّهُ عَلَيْهِ وَسَلَّم: خذ خاتمك انتفع به. قال: لا والله لا آخذه أبداً وقد طرحه رَسُولِ اللَّهِ صَلَّى اللَّهُ عَلَيْهِ وَسَلَّم

"The Messenger of Allah *SAAW* saw a person with a gold signet ring on his hand. He pulled it off and threw it away saying, 'One of you is bringing a piece of fire from hell and putting it on his hand.' After Allah's Messenger *SAAW* had left, someone said to the man, 'Take your ring and derive benefit out of it,' whereupon the man replied, 'I would never take it after Allah's Messenger *SAAW* has thrown it away.'"[95]

The above examples clearly show that the Prophet *SAAW* illustrated the consequences of bad deeds in a very vivid way so that they would have a lasting impact on his Companions and would stay alive in their minds. This way, he *SAAW* made sure that his Companions strictly followed his instructions and guidance.

Parents should try to use this principle with their teens, rather than just telling them, "No, you can't do this," or "That is *haram*."

94. Bukhari
95. Muslim

Here are a few **examples** of how parents can apply this principle with their children.

If a child becomes lazy and does not do his homework properly or complete his assigned tasks, his parent can sit down with him and discuss the issue in a quiet way, trying to convince him that it is important for his future that he work hard so he can be a person of value and be able to hold down a job. After this, if his behavior is still not up to par, the parent can take him downtown and show him some of the homeless people on the streets. Ask him if this is how he would like to live in the future. Tell him this might be what happens if he neglects his work and does not do what it takes to become a successful person.

If a young child refuses to brush her teeth, parents should talk to her about it and try to convince her that it is important for her hygiene. If she still will not do it, the parent should let the child go with him on errands, and stop by a pharmacy to pick up a few things. The parent can make sure to stop in the aisle where dentures are displayed. The parent can let the child notice the dentures, and explain to her that this is what happens to people who don't take care of their teeth. Their teeth rot and fall out, and then the people need to wear fake teeth that really hurt for the rest of their lives

Chapter 27

Use a Holistic Approach

Islam approaches the question of *tarbiyah* of human beings in a holistic way. It touches every angle of the human being to make sure that this *tarbiyah* produces well-rounded individuals who are justly balanced and moderate in their behaviour. In *Surah al-Baqarah*, Allah *SWT* says:

"يَا أَيُّهَا الَّذِينَ آمَنُواْ ادْخُلُواْ فِي السِّلْمِ كَآفَّةً وَلاَ تَتَّبِعُواْ خُطُوَاتِ الشَّيْطَانِ إِنَّهُ لَكُمْ عَدُوٌّ مُّبِينٌ"

"Oh you who believe, enter Islam in totality and don't follow the footsteps of *Shaytan*, for he is an open enemy to you."[96]

In the same *surah*, the Qur'an talks about those who believe in some parts of the scripture but not others by describing them in a very humiliating way, and by promising them severe punishment. It says:

"أَفَتُؤْمِنُونَ بِبَعْضِ الْكِتَابِ وَتَكْفُرُونَ بِبَعْضٍ فَمَا جَزَاء مَن يَفْعَلُ ذَلِكَ مِنكُمْ إِلاَّ خِزْيٌ فِي الْحَيَاةِ الدُّنْيَا وَيَوْمَ الْقِيَامَةِ يُرَدُّونَ إِلَى أَشَدِّ الْعَذَابِ وَمَا اللّهُ بِغَافِلٍ عَمَّا تَعْمَلُونَ"

"Is it only a part of the book that you believe in, and you reject the rest? The reward of those among you who behave like this is disgrace in this life, and on the Day of Judgment you will be given the most grievous penalty, for Allah is not unmindful of what you do."[97]

---

96. (Q2, V208)
97. (Q2, V85)

This is an indication that Muslims should take Islam as a complete package. We should not pick and choose only what is convenient and easy to apply and leave behind other issues that may cause us some inconvenience.

One of the common mistakes of parents in North America is the unbalanced approach in *tarbiyah*. For example, some emphasize the issue of wearing *hijab* with their daughters and do nothing else to prepare the child for this change. Yes, wearing *hijab* is important, but making sure that the child is convinced that it is the right thing to do is even more important. Using a comprehensive and well-rounded approach to *tarbiyah* is necessary to obtain the desired results. Islam respects thinking and encourages us to question in order to reach the right conclusion and understand the reasoning behind certain prohibitions. Forcing a child to do something without convincing him that it is the right thing to do can be very costly in the future, when the child becomes an adult and has the right to choose his way without the parents' intervention.

To avoid this, parents should make sure that their approach to tarbiyah is a well-rounded one. It should cover various aspects and meet the child's various needs. Using stories, videos, Islamic camps, conferences and other tools is very helpful in this. Parents should be careful not to over-emphasize one subject and neglect other areas of *tarbiyah*. They should focus not only on filling the child's mind with knowledge, because this alone will not have an impact on the child's behaviour, but they must also focus on teaching the child to implement what she has learned. Theory by itself has very little value without practice, especially considering that we will be rewarded only for what we practice and not for what we know.

One story that stresses this concept is about a religious scholar who was approached by several of his students. They came to tell him about a man that they knew who had memorized all of the *ahadith* in *Sahih al-Bukhari*. The scholar observed the man's behaviour for several days, and sadly noticed that his knowledge of the *ahadith* seemed to have no effect on his character. The scholar then returned to his students and told them that now, they all had an extra copy of *Sahih Al-Bukhari*.

As parents, we do not want our child to be an extra copy of *Sahih al-Bukhari*, or even an extra copy of the Qur'an. It is much more valuable for the child to understand and apply the knowledge that he learns. This concept is stressed by Abdullah Ibn Mas'oud *RAA*, who said, "We used to learn the Qur'an ten verses at a time. We would memorize them, act upon them, and then move on to the next ten verses. And thus we learned the knowledge and applied it at the same time."

Another indication of the importance of implementing what we have learned is the Prophet's behaviour *SAAW*, as explained in the following *hadith*:

"دخلت على عائشة فسألتها عن أخلاق رسول الله صلى الله عليه وسلم فقالت:
كان خلقه القرآن"

> "When 'A'isha *RAA* was asked about the Prophet's character, she replied, 'His manners were the Qur'an,'[98] which means that he practiced everything that he learned from the Qur'an."

There are various ways that parents can take a holistic approach to teaching Islam to their children. Modeling, for example, is a good technique to use regardless of the child's age, because when children see their parents following certain rules or engaging in certain behaviours, it leaves a lasting effect on them. In this way, parents can lead by example.

Another extremely important approach is dialogue. Parents should avoid simply lecturing to their children about what is right and wrong. Instead, they should discuss the reasoning behind the rules and give their children a chance to ask questions in an open

98. Muslim

environment. This approach is particularly effective with teenagers, who will be unlikely to follow rules without being convinced of their importance. Also, by providing an environment that allows and encourages dialogue, parents give their teens a chance to ask questions and learn more about Islam than if they were simply lectured at and not given the chance to ask questions.

Chapter 28

Control Your Anger

Among the greatest advice of the Prophet *SAAW* is to not be angry.

عن أبي هريرة قال: جاء رجل إلى النبي صلى الله عليه وسلم فقال: مرني ولا تكثر فلعلي أعقله فقال: لا تغضب. فأعاد عليه فقال: لا تغضب

"Abu Hurairah *RAA* narrated that a man asked the Messenger of Allah *SAAW* to give him a piece of advice. He *SAAW* said, 'Do not be angry.' The man repeated his question several times, and each time the Prophet *SAAW* replied, 'Do not be angry.'"[99]

The following is another *hadith* that addresses anger.

"ليس الشديد بالصرعة ولكن الشديد الذي يملك نفسه عند الغضب"

In this hadith, the Prophet *SAAW* defined the strongest person as the one who controls himself when he is in a fit of rage, not as the one who wrestles others.[100]

Mu'ath Ibn Anas *RAA* narrated that the Prophet *SAAW* said:

"من كظم غيظا وهو يستطيع أن ينفذه دعاه الله يوم القيامة على رؤوس الخلائق حتى يخيره في أي الحور شاء"

"The one who swallows up anger will be called out by Allah, the Exalted, to the forefront of the creatures on the Day of Resurrection and will be allowed to choose any pure-eyed virgin, he would like."[101]

---

99. Bukhari
100. Agreed upon
101. Abu Dawud and Tirrmidhi

Not only did the Prophet *SAAW* warn us against becoming angry, but he also taught us the best anger management techniques:

• Seek refuge with Allah *SWT* from Satan.

Suliman Ibn Surd *RAA* reported that:

استب رجلان عند النبي صلى الله عليه وسلم فاشتد غضب أحدهما فقال النبي صلى الله عليه وسلم: "إني لأعلم كلمة لو قالها لذهب عنه الغضب. أعوذ بالله من الشيطان الرجيم. فقال الرجل أمجنون تراني؟ فتلا رسول الله صلى الله عليه وسلم: "وإما ينزغنك من الشيطان نزغ فاستعذ بالله من الشيطان الرجيم"

> "Two people began to quarrel with each other in front of the Prophet *SAAW*. One of them was so angry that his face turned red and the veins in his neck were swollen. The Messenger of Allah *SAAW* said, 'I know of a phrase that, if he were to utter it, would relax his fit of rage, and that phrase is: 'I seek refuge with Allah from Satan, the accursed.' The man said: 'Do you think I'm crazy?' The prophet *SAAW* recited verse 36 of *Surah Fussilat* 'When you find the evil whisper of satan influencing you, seek refuge with Allah.'"[102]

• Change your position: It was narrated that the Messenger of Allah *SAAW* said:

"إذا غضب أحدكم وهو قائم فليجلس فإن ذهب عنه الغضب وإلا فليضطجع"

> "If one of you gets angry while he is standing, let him sit down, and if he is still angry, let him lie down."[103]

102. Agreed upon
103. Ahmad

• Perform *wudu'*: It was narrated that the Prophet *SAAW* said:

"إن الغضب من الشيطان وإن الشيطان خلق من النار وإنما تطفأ النار بالماء فإذا غضب أحدكم فليتوضأ"

"Anger is from Satan and Satan is created from fire, and fire is extinguished by water; so if one of you becomes angry let him perform *wudu'*."[104]

• Be silent: It was narrated that the Prophet *SAAW* said:

"إذا غضب أحدكم فليسكت"

"If one of you becomes angry, let him be silent."[105]

Parents should use all these wonderful techniques to manage their anger when they are in a conflict with their children. They should not be quick to react when they are upset with their teens, but should use one of the above strategies instead. It may be difficult at first, and it does take training, but these techniques are very helpful and make it a lot easier to avoid unnecessary, added problems. Parents should also teach their children these anger management techniques, and train them to practice them as well.

Here is a practical **example** of how a parent can apply these anger management techniques in case of a conflict with his child:

Suppose that the child has broken a rule and her parent is very angry about it. Instead of shouting, yelling, and accusing the child of never following the rules, the parent must not rush to react or vent his anger. He should try to control his anger by using one of the above techniques, such as staying quiet or making *wudu'*. He should also tell the child, in a firm but calm voice, that he will discuss what has happened after both of them have calmed down. The parent should mention to the child that he is going

104. Abu Dawud

105. Ahmad

to make *wudu'* because the Prophet *SAAW* taught us to do this, and suggest to the child that she should do the same.

After both the parent and the child have calmed down, the parent should start the dialogue with his child, giving her the opportunity to describe what happened from her point of view. He must listen to her openly, and then explain why her behavior was wrong and that she should not have done it. The parent must make sure to remain calm and respectful during this dialogue, and remember that he is not only trying to solve the problem, but is also modeling for the child the Islamic way to resolve conflicts. If the situation requires the parent to take disciplinary action by, for example, depriving her of certain privileges as a consequence of her mistake, then the parent must not hesitate to carry out the punishment. However, he must make sure that the child understands the reason for the punishment and that she does not simply view it as her parent's angry reaction to her behavior.

CHAPTER 29

TEACH THEM *HAYA'*

It was reported that the Prophet *SAAW* said:

"إن لكل دين خلقا، وإن خلق الإسلام الحياء"

"For every *deen*, there is a main characteristic, and the characteristic of Islam is *hayaa'*."[106]

Also, the Prophet *SAAW* was described as having more *hayaa'* than a virgin who stays in her own private room out of shyness, rather than going out in public. Although *haaya'* is usually translated as modesty, it is certainly much more than that. It is shyness, bashfulness, and complete avoidance of any obscene talk or actions.

North American culture does not promote *hayaa'* at all. Most news magazines, TV programs and even commercials are full of unacceptable scenes that promote obscenity and low moral values. The norms for acceptable behavior are rapidly expanding and becoming the worst they have ever been. As Muslims, we should not follow the crowd or accept these norms. It is absolutely critical that parents protect their children from the low level of morality that is fully acceptable in North American society. The episode between U.S. President Bill Clinton and Monica Lewinsky attests to this low level of morality. Even after her testimony and his confession, 62% of the U.S. population still saw nothing wrong with what their president did. How low can the level of morality go?

---

106. Ibn Majah

CHAPTER 30

DO NOT FORCE THEM TO PICK UP WHERE YOU LEFT OFF

Parents have to consider what stage their child is at. They should not ask him to do things that are beyond his current level. 'A'isha *RAA* is reported to have said, "Take into consideration the young girl's age." Some parents, in their zeal and enthusiasm to have their children behave, act, and dress as Muslims, insist on forcing their teens to do exactly as they do. For **example**, a mother might ask her teenage daughter to dress exactly as she does, in a full *jilbab* and *khimar*. However, there is nothing wrong with accepting loose clothing and a scarf as the daughter's *hijab* at this stage, even if it is not exactly like her mom's clothing. As long as the girl's clothing meets the Islamic requirements, parents should accept it. The basic requirements call for the clothes to cover the whole body, not to be tight or transparent, and to cover the head.

Another common **example** is when a father asks his son to pray all the extra prayers, such as the full *taraweeh* during Ramadan, and to dress in his country's traditional dress, thinking that this is the only way to apply Islam. There is nothing wrong with accepting only the compulsory duties from the young man and helping him to grow and strengthen his belief gradually in the meantime. This way, the son will be able to do the extra things without feeling that it is too much of a burden on him. In some situations, if a teen is forced to do more and more without having any real conviction, he may completely turn away from Islam. Therefore, we have to take the child's age into consideration and give him enough room to grow.

One way that may help parents exercise this principle is to try to remember whether or not they were fully applying Islam when they were their child's age. Of course, most parents' answer to this question is **no**. Therefore, parents should give their teen enough time to grow, develop, and gradually improve day after day. When parents encourage and praise their teen's positive actions, instead of being critical of him, he will do more and more things correctly, insha'Allah. This is exactly what the Prophet *SAAW* did with his Companions. He accepted what they did according to their level, and then helped them to improve. Not only this, but he also applauded and praised their positive actions, even if the actions were little or seemed irrelevant. Here is an incident confirming this:

جاء أعرابي من نجد ثائر الرأس (مضاف والتقدير ثائر شعر الرأس أي قائمة منتشرة) يسمع دوي صوته ولا يفقه ما يقول حتى إذا دنا فإذا هو يسأل عن الإسلام فقال له النبي صلى اللّه عليه وسلم: " خَمْسُ صَلَوَاتٍ فِي الْيَوْمِ وَاللَّيْلَةِ ".قال هل عليّ غيرها؟ قال: "لاَ.الاَّ أَنْ تَطَوَّعَ."وذكر له النبي صلى اللّه عليه اللّه وسلم صيام شهر رمضان فقال: هل عليّ غيره؟ قال: "لاَ.الاَّ أَنْ تَطَوَّعَ." فأدبر الرجل وهو يقول واللّه لا أزيد على هذا ولا أنقص منه شيئاً. فقال رسول اللّه صلى اللّه عليه وسلم: "أفلح ان صدق"

> "It was reported that a man came to the Prophet *SAAW* and asked him about Islam. The Prophet *SAAW* told him about the basic pillars of Islam (five daily prayers, *zakah*, fasting). The man said he would do only this and nothing more. The Prophet *SAAW* said that this man would achieve prosperity if he implemented what he said he would."[107]

In *Surah al-Baqarah*, Allah *SWT* says:

"لاَ يُكَلِّفُ اللّهُ نَفْسًا إِلاَّ وُسْعَهَا"

"Allah does not burden any soul beyond its capability."[108]

107. Musnad Al-Imam Al-Shafi'i

108. (Q2, V286)

The Prophet *SAAW* also said:

"فما أمرتكم به من شيء فأتوا منه ما استطعتم وما نهيتكم عنه فانتهوا"

"Do your best in what I have commanded you to do and avoid completely what I have prohibited."[109]

Using this gradual approach is very important and is a fundamental method used by Islam to introduce new concepts and to change social habits. It is much easier for teens to make changes gradually than abruptly.

109. Tabarani

Arabic Terminology

Most Islamic books contain Arabic terms that are frequently used throughout the books. These words seem to constitute a basic vocabulary that must be available to the reader. In the following glossary of Arabic terms, we attempt to provide most of the terms used in this book with their definitions.

Term	Definition
adhaan	The call to prayer
ahadith	Plural of *hadith*; The collection of the sayings of the Prophet Muhammad *SAAW*
alhamdulillah	All praise is due to Allah *SWT*
Ansar	Supporters. Usually refers to the Muslims of the city of Medina, who supported the Prophet *SAAW*
aqeedah	Islamic creed
'asr	The third daily prayer, at mid-afternoon
athkar	Plural of *thikr*
Bedouin	A person from the Arabian desert
da'wah	Call or mission. It usually refers to calling others to folllow Allah's way
deen	Way of life. Relgion. Usually refers to the religion of Islam.
dhuhr	The second daily prayer, at noon
dinar	An old, valuable currency, made of gold, used by Arabs
dirham	An old currency, made of silver or copper, used by Arabs. It is worth less than a *dinar*
du'a	Supplication
'Eid	The Muslim celebration after the month of *Ramadan* and after the time of pilgrimage
fajr	Dawn. Usually applies to the first obligatory prayer of the day, after dawn but before sunrise

fawahish	Shameful deeds
fiqh	The ability to understand and derive rules and regula tions from existing texts and evidence for practical Islamic applications and regulations related to the immediate environment
hadith	Reports of the Prophet's sayings, actions, and approvals
halal	Allowed or permitted, according to Islam
haram	Forbidden or prohibited, according to Islam
hayaa'	Decency, modesty, bashfulness, morality, and humility
hijab	Muslim women's proper dress. It covers everything except the face and hands. It could take any form as long as it meets the requirement of being loose so that it does not describe the body details and of being non-transparent
halaqa	Circle. Usually refers to a study circle
ihsan	The process of perfecting one's deeds. According to the *hadith* of the Prophet *SAAW*, it means to worship Allah *SWT* as if you see Him, and if you don't see Him, knowing that He sees you
iman	Faith, level of belief
insha'Allah	God willing
'isha	The fifth daily prayer, after the sun has set, twilight is gone, and night has fallen (i.e., when the sky is completely dark)
istikhara	A specific prayer used to ask Allah *SWT* to guide you to make the right decision regarding any issue
itikaf	Seclusion. Usually refers to the act of staying in the mosque longer than the regular time for prayers, for the purpose of worshipping. Although it may be done at any time, it is practiced more by Muslims during the month of *Ramadan*

jannah	Paradise, Heaven
jilbab	A loose, one-piece dress that covers the whole body
khimar	A large, loose one-piece scarf that covers a woman's head as well as the shoulders and may reach down to the waist
maghrib	*The fourth daily prayer, at sunset*
masha'Allah	Literally, "Whatever Allah wills." Usually used as an expression of admiration or glorification of Allah for something that is very pleasing or that has been done well.
mohasabah	The process of reviewing, assessing, and evaluating your deeds regularly to ensure that they are as close to Allah's orders as possible
nafl	Extra. Usually refers to an extra act of worship, beyond the obligatory and *sunnan* acts, which a Muslim may voluntarily do to get closer to Allah
nawafel	Plural of *nafl*
niqab	A woman's veil that covers the face
Ramadan	The ninth month of the Islamic calendar. Muslims must fast from dawn to sunset during this month
Sahaaba	Plural of *Sahaabi*
Sahaabi	A Companion of the Prophet *SAAW*
Salaf	The third generation of Muslims, after the *Sahaaba* and the *Tabi'in.*
seerah	The biography of the Prophet Muhammad *SAAW*
Shaytan	Satan
subhanallah	How perfect is Allah
sunnah	Way, teaching, or guidance. In the Islamic context, it always refers to the guidance provided to Muslims by the Prophet Muhammad *SAAW*
sunnan	Plural of *sunnah*

surah/surat	Chapter of the Qur'an
Tabi'in	The second generation of Muslims, after the *Sahaaba*
tafseer	Explanation or interpretation of the Qur'an
tarbiyah	The art of dealing with human nature by guiding people to make the right decisions and to improve by gently coaching and training to make sure that they are close to Allah, that they make the right decision and become bettter people.
tazkiah	The process of purification. Usually refers to purifying the soul through extra acts of worship and remembrance of Allah
tazkiatu annafs	The process of purifying the soul
thikr	Remembering Allah through words, meditation, and reflection
ummah	Community
wudu'	Ablution. Performed by Muslims before *salah.*
zakah	Growth. The religious definition is *obligatory charity*

References

———. *The Noble Qur'an, English Translation of the Meanings and Commentary*. Medina, Kingdom of Saudi Arabia: King Fahd Complex for the Printing of the Holy Qur'an, 1417 A.H.

Beshir, Dr. Ekram and Mohamed Rida Beshir. *Meeting the Challenge of Parenting in the West, An Islamic Perspective, second edition.* Beltsville, Maryland: Amana Publications, 2000.

Beshir, Drs. Ekram and Mohamed Rida Beshir. *Muslim Teens: Today's Worry, Tomorrow's Hope, first edition.* Beltsville, Maryland: Amana Publications, 2001.

Imam Abi Al-Husain Muslim Ibn Al-Haggag Al-Qushairee Al-Naisabouree *Sahih Muslim, first edition,* Cairo: *Dar Ihiaa' Alkutob Alarabia,* 1955.

Imam Abi Abdellah Muhammad Ibn Ismail Ibn Ibraheem Ibn Al-Mogheirah Ibn Bardezabah Al-Bukhari, *Sahih al-Bukhari,*Cairo, *Dar Al Shaa'b.*

Imam Al-Hafez Abi Dawud Sulaiman Ibn Al-Asha'th Al-Sagestany Al-Azdei *Sunan Aby Dawud, first edition,* Bayroot, *Dar Ibn Hazm,* 1998.

Imam Al-Hafez Aby Abderahaman Ahmad Ibn Shua'ib Ibn Ali Ibn Senan Ibn Dinar Al-Nisa'i *Sunan Al-Nisa'i, first edition,* Bayroot, *Dar Ibn Hazm,* 1999.

Imam Ibn Majah *Sunan Ibn Majah, first edition,* Cairo, *Dar Ihiaa'At Turath Al-A'raby*, 1975

Other books of Hadith, *"Ahmad, Tabarani, Tirmidhi,..."*

Shaykh Muhammad Al-Ghazaly, *Muslim Character, first edition, Salimiah, Kuwait, International Islamic Federation of Student Organizations, 1983*

Shaykh Abdul Fattah Abu Ghudda, *Islamic manners, Swansea, U.K., Awakening Publications, 2001*